# NO BOSS!

The Real Truth about Working Independently:
12 Lessons from 30 Years of Bossing Myself Around

## STEVEN CRISTOL

*No Boss! The Real Truth about Working Independently: 12 Lessons from 30 Years of Bossing Myself Around* Copyright © 2022 Steven M. Cristol

All rights reserved.

No part of this book may be reproduced or used in any form or by any electronic or mechanical means, including information storage and retrieval systems, without prior written permission from the copyright owner, except for use of brief quotations in book reviews.

Book and cover design: Vladimir Verano, Vetvolta Design

ISBN 979-8-9859290-0-3 (Paperback Edition)
ISBN 979-8-9859290-1-0 (eBook Edition)

Library of Congress Control Number 2022904634

Printed and bound in the United States of America
First printing: September, 2022

Strategic Harmony Books
Permissions contact: permissions@noboss.me

Excerpt from *Gifts of the Jews*, © 1998 by Thomas Cahill, reprinted by permission of Doubleday, a division of Penguin Random House.

To Lee Franklin, whose wisdom, generosity, and friendship have informed my work life—and this book—in myriad ways. He has modeled the best of what independent work can be.

# Author's Note:
# Work And The Pandemic

I began planning this book shortly before the Covid-19 pandemic swept across our planet. It seems like long ago: B.C.—Before Covid. In those days, working from home was, for some, an idealized fantasy. But for the overwhelming majority of employed people, it was impractical. For others, undesirable. For most full-time workers, regardless of appeal, it was certainly not normal.

Then came lockdowns and social distancing, and Zoom became a household word as teleconferencing from home quickly became pervasive. Suddenly there was collective whiplash among the employed: instead of needing permission to work from home, permission was needed to enter the workplace. Many companies announced that they would permanently relinquish some office space because employees had proven that working remotely could be sufficiently productive. Before the pandemic, Americans spent five percent of their working time at home; by mid-2020 it was more than 60 percent. In Japan, where company employees working from home was almost unthinkable B.C., more than 30 percent were doing it by mid-2020. Similar stories echoed in developed economies around the world.

At that point I had to revisit pre-pandemic assumptions that led me to write this book. After all, with millions of people having wondered what it would be like to be their own boss and, in many cases, work from home independently, some of the book's value would be to illuminate what to expect from the latter. Now, A.C.—

After Covid—so many people have experienced working from home that much of the mystery and wonderment has dissipated.

I (briefly!) considered scrapping the book when the pandemic was at its worst. Then, as we entered our second Covid year, survey data began to show the degree to which working from home was a polarizing experience. Many enjoyed their increased independence, the pause in commuting, and more flexibility to attend to family matters. And many actually increased their productivity. But for many others, the cons—not least of which were deep feelings of isolation and loneliness—outweighed the pros so much that nearly one third of employed workers banned from their workplaces considered quitting their jobs. Either way, well beyond the issue of workplace, Covid provoked heightened levels of soul-searching about the nature of work and its enormous place in the contemporary human experience.

Such introspection, it turns out, along with Covid-driven societal and economic disruption, fertilized the need for this book. Even after a pandemic has pushed us closer to life's biggest questions, few things require more self-examination than deciding to be your own boss. The book's real value has much more to do with working independently than with working from home. In some endeavors, the two are tightly intertwined. But in most, *where* the work is done is so much less important to satisfaction than *what* the work is, to what degree it provides meaning and joy, and what it means to be your own boss. Those are the primary themes herein. So the book survives. I hope you'll be glad it did.

# Contents

Prelude     *1*

## PART I
## SETTING EXPECTATIONS AND CHOOSING YOUR PATH

Lesson #1
Don't Assume Your New Boss Will Be Better than Your Old Boss    *7*

Lesson #2
Know Your Motives (and Be Honest with Yourself!)    *15*

Lesson #3
Make a Disciplined Choice among the Many Paths to Independence    *22*

Lesson #4
Confront Who You Really Are Before Taking the Plunge    *34*

## PART II
## MAKING IT HAPPEN

Lesson #5
See Perfectionism for the Curse That It Is    *47*

Lesson #6
Get the Help You Need Even If You Think You Don't Need It    *55*

Lesson #7
Choose and Manage Relationships Carefully    *64*

Lesson #8
Give Yourself Performance Reviews    *78*

Lesson #9
Know When to End a Marriage (to an Idea)    *91*

## PART III
## SUSTAINING INDEPENDENT SUCCESS

Lesson #10
Making It Work for the Long Haul    *103*

Lesson #11
Independence as a Gateway to a Larger Life    *112*

Lesson #12
Lessons from Others    *118*

## Coda

Your Signing Ceremony for the No Boss Contract    *139*

## Acknowledgements and Gratitude    *144*

## About the Author    *147*

# Prelude

◆

You're the boss! *Now what?*

It may seem obvious that this is the crucial space for your mind to inhabit before venturing out on your own, whether to start a company or hang out a shingle as an expert. But the first time I left a very good job to do just that, at age 28, I had thought a lot more about the first part of "You're the boss! Now what?" than the second part.

This is not a book about how to build a business (though it will help!). It is not a book about business strategy, writing a business plan, researching your customers, or turning your idea into a wildly successful major corporation. Nor is it a book about how to get rich—at least not in monetary terms. What it is is a book about knowing if independent work is a good fit for you, acting on a dream, and increasing the odds of positive outcomes. It's also a book for those already on the independent path who want their work to be less stressful, more productive and more satisfying. For those of you not yet working independently but frustrated by your current or recent employment experience, it's a book about saying goodbye to soul-sucking work for someone else and replacing it with some balance of purpose, fulfillment, self-sufficiency, freedom, and—oh, yes—livelihood.

If you're gainfully employed now (or only temporarily unemployed) and have ever sat in a staff meeting or at your desk, or stood on the floor while working in a company factory or retail store, and found yourself staring into space and fantasizing about working for yourself, this book is for you. It's a window on the world of being your own boss, through which I simply share the things I have learned and wish I had known ahead of 30-plus years of self-employment. It's about the emotional and financial ups and downs, and the joys and scars from re-inventing one's self multiple times, with a frame of reference informed by my previous full-time employment at five companies earlier in my career.

Of course all those companies had bosses. *Many* bosses. I've been near the bottom (in two mid-sized companies in the early years), and closer to the top (vice president in both a Fortune 100 company with more than 60,000 employees and a venture-backed Silicon Valley startup as employee #35). I had a total of nine bosses in those five companies (and several other senior executives who presumed they were also my bosses, and acted like it). In between and afterwards, I've had a tenth boss: *me*, for a total now of more than three decades. But more about that tenth boss's mistakes later, and learning from them. By the way—I'm not done; I'm still working, still bossing myself around.

First, a confession: this is not the book I originally intended to write. It was supposed to be my third book on business strategy. I holed up in a cabin in the San Juan Islands in the U.S. Pacific Northwest for two weeks to jumpstart the writing of that book. But when I opened my laptop on the first day to step into the ring again with a blank page, I found myself gazing out the window and thinking about the long journey—how I came to be in that particular place on that particular day.

It was a place of great natural beauty, with shimmering salt water lapping up on the sand in front of the cabin, and my trusty old sea kayak resting on the deck competing for my attention with the same pull as a young child asking Daddy to come out and play in the snow. How lucky I was to be there instead of sitting in a boring meeting or working on a boss's pet project that I didn't believe in. I heard myself laugh out loud as I exulted in my freedom.

But then I also thought about how hard it had been. And I cried a little too, reflecting on some of the leaner times and getting up every morning all those years knowing I wouldn't earn a dollar unless I made something happen that day that people would value enough to pay for. In my case, there was no physical product to sell—just walking into prospective clients' offices empty-handed except for some knowledge and experience, listening skills, and a strong desire to help. But fundamentally naked.

Like life itself, self-employment is nothing if not a mixed bag. The trade-offs are endless, and there is no owner's manual specific to you. I'm quite sure I wasted hundreds of hours in the first half of my self-employment years trying to get it right. But I've thought deeply about how and why. And as George Harrison sang, "With every mistake we must surely be learning." Many days served up a big dose of humility to build upon. Self-employment is not for sissies.

Yet when I now think about the privilege of having advised so many great companies, having had the opportunity to write a couple of successful business books and earn a patent for a business decision model, and having had the flexibility to go back to school mid-career to study music and get songs of mine recorded by well-known artists, the experience has certainly been net positive. I see these achievements as very modest in comparison to luminaries both in and outside the business world, so this book focuses instead on alerting you to potholes I stepped in, false assumptions I made, things I could have done better or differently, and shortcuts to things that I only figured out later in my journey. And I've tried to keep it general enough to be useful to you no matter what kind of self-employment adventure you're contemplating or have already undertaken.

I've also tried to keep it short; if you're successful in independent work, you'll be busy! And if you choose not to be quite that busy (like I've chosen on occasional Tuesdays when the beckoning of my guitar or the nearby ocean was too much to resist), you'll want the extra time for fun and relaxation. And speaking of fun, I'm weary of humorless business books (including my own previous ones), so I'm determined that this one will provide at least a few smiles along the way.

Finally—and this is *crucial*—since working independently is not for everyone, this book does not pre-suppose that self-employment will be good for *you*. I do, however, try to give you a big leg up in anticipating if it is or isn't. I will raise the question more than once as to whether you're cut out for successful self-employment. Much better to find out now than after cutting the cord on a dependable livelihood with paying work that may not be perfect but is significantly better than tolerable. Just because self-employeds as a percentage of total workforce continues to rise rapidly, especially with the emerging gig economy, that doesn't mean it's a good choice for you. The tale of lemmings following each other only to throw themselves off cliffs and drown in the sea is a myth, but the fact that they do get eaten in large quantities by foxes and weasels is not.

So let's acknowledge up front that there's a big world of fulfillment and rewards in working for someone else under the right circumstances. My hope is that, if you're in those circumstances, the book will help you more fully appreciate them, alert you to what you may be giving up and signing up for by leaving, and quell your wanderlust—or even help you to more fully scratch your entrepreneurial itch inside an existing organization without having to leave. But if that's not you, this is the book I wish someone had handed me all those years ago when I told my boss that I was quitting and heading out to uncharted seas.

Bon voyage, and may the winds be at your back!

# PART I

♦

# Setting Expectations and Choosing Your Path

# LESSON 1

◆

## Don't Assume Your New Boss Will Be Better than Your Old Boss

◆

*"By working faithfully eight hours a day you may eventually get to be boss and work twelve hours a day."*
~ Robert Frost

*"I particularly like the whole thing of being boss. Boss and employee … It's the slave quality that I find very alluring."*
~ Hugh Grant

I was lucky—I had some great bosses. I know this because I also had two bosses who could have been the inspiration for the movie *Horrible Bosses*. Nothing makes you appreciate a great boss like a horrible boss. Regardless of your own experience to date, it's easy to assume that you'll be kinder, more compassionate, and more reasonable than your last boss when you're bossing yourself around. Don't be so sure. My own cautionary tale is a case in point.

By the time I had 50 people reporting to me in a large company, I had studied the differences between great and horrible bosses. I truly wanted to be a great boss and worked very hard at it. When I started that job, I quickly learned that some bureaucratic lapses had left several members of my team without performance reviews for more than two years. I promised they would all have one by year end. I couldn't know that before year end I would have a massive disk herniation and be hospitalized with spinal surgery, followed by a 10-week mandatory recuperation away from the office. In mid-December, however, when I couldn't yet sit comfortably in a chair, I went to the office for the first time since surgery and gave all seven of my direct reports their performance reviews, back-to-back in one very long day—with me lying flat on the floor throughout. (Nothing says "boss" like having each of your direct reports looking down at you at their feet.) Okay, I admit that was a little off the deep end. But a promise is a promise.

Two years later, on the day I left the company, my employees presented me with a surprise gift: a beautiful leather-bound book. In it was a collection of handwritten letters from every member of my team telling me what the experience of working for me had meant to them. I was deeply moved, eyes moist, feeling at that moment like a great boss. But I initially overlooked the very dark side of all that—a flashing warning sign that I should have seen about setting boundaries. We'll get to that in Lesson 8. There we might decide that maybe I wasn't such a great boss after all when we consider that leather-bound book's implications for working independently.

That brings us to the Jekyll-and-Hyde part of the story. It's easy to forget when you're stepping out on your own that you'll not only be the boss but also his/her/their[1] subordinate. There's no escaping that you'll be the one bossed around by your inner boss. Especially after having received those beautiful letters from my employees, I was not prepared for what I quickly discovered when I started working for myself (and then kept discovering over and over again): that the nice guy I thought I was actually had the capacity to be—pardon the expression—a complete sonofabitch as the boss of myself. Unreasonably demanding. Relentlessly hypercritical. Mercilessly unforgiving. Need I go on?

No, so let's talk about you. You may be surprised by yourself too.

## Pushing Yourself

Now that there's no one else to push you, you'll be doing that yourself. Fortunately, nothing helps here like that inescapable feeling

---

[1] Please choose your own pronouns throughout this book; my tendency to use he and she belies my belief in honoring self-determined gender identity.

that "now it's *all* up to me." Trouble is, while that feeling is the mother of all motivators, it's also a trap.

Yes, your old boss pushed you. "That big report I needed by Friday afternoon I now need by Wednesday. Wednesday *morning*." But one thing you had going for you then is that you never completely 100% trusted your boss. So there was natural questioning, doubt, resistance—because a boss is something to push back against, even if you only do it in your mind. But when you're your own boss, there's a tendency to trust yourself without that resistance. *That's the trap.* Since you probably believe that you wouldn't purposely do yourself harm, you can find yourself almost mindlessly following your own orders every day without questioning them. Without pushing back. And before you know it, your new boss is running you ragged, believing that the harder s/he pushes the more successful you'll be. Chances are you'll even find out that the new boss is even stingier with vacation time than with expenses. And that's *really* stingy.

So to keep you from quickly going from self-employed to self-annoyed, it's good to set out some ground rules in the beginning. *I recommend that you and your new boss sign a contract*—yes, seriously—which, conveniently, will now only require one signature to cover both of you. Subsequent chapters will further explain and dissect these ground rules, or *covenants* (as I like to think of them), and reveal their importance. (Also conveniently, Covenants 1 through 9 below are each covered in the corresponding chapter number. The last four covenants are covered in the book's final Part III.)

## Your New (Self-)Employment Contract

The No Boss Contract starts with "We the undersigned agree," and *you* are *we* (boss and subordinate). It looks like this:

> We, the undersigned, agree to the following covenants:
>
> *Covenant 1.* We will develop daily mindfulness of the dynamic between internal boss and internal subordinate to quality-control the relationship for mutual benefit.

*Covenant 2.* We will both be aligned and very clear on the reasons why we want to work independently or start a new business, and will thoughtfully and honestly commit those reasons to writing—in priority order of importance, and before we commence (if we haven't already started).

*Covenant 3.* We will rationalize the path to independence that we choose by disciplined evaluation of alternatives in the context of the reasons articulated in Covenant 2.

*Covenant 4.* We will ensure, before taking the independent plunge (or even if already taken), that the path forward reflects our most authentic self—at least for who we really are right now.

*Covenant 5.* We will diligently monitor the presence of perfectionism that is out of proportion to the task at hand, call it out when we see it, and adjust behavior accordingly.

*Covenant 6.* We will get the help we need before the lack of it materially degrades our performance, our capacity, and/or our mental or physical well-being.

*Covenant 7.* We will choose and manage our external business relationships with the utmost attention not only to strategic fit but also to their net impact on both the internal boss and subordinate, personally and professionally, and always in the context of highest ethical standards.

*Covenant 8.* We will give ourselves a performance review (as prescribed in Lesson 8) at reasonable intervals, in which both the internal boss and subordinate can productively check in on how they are doing in the other's eyes and in their own.

Covenant 9. We will have the courage down the line and at intervals thereafter to ask and answer whether our original business idea for working independently is still the best idea for our well-being—or whether we need a different (or substantially modified) dream.

*Covenant 10.* We will consider the management and persistent reduction of worry as an essential daily pillar of productive work.

*Covenant 11.* We will strive to master the counterintuitive art of resting as a strategy for success.

*Covenant 12.* We will further develop the art of both living and working in gratitude, which will nourish our work and all other covenants.

*Covenant 13.* We will not forget that even independent businesses need a "social license to operate" which is earned by responsible behavior that positively impacts the greater good.

Print name: _____<br>
Signature: _____<br>
Date: _____

It would of course be unreasonable to ask you to sign before finishing the book. I'll gently remind you at the end. Or maybe not so gently. Let's just say that, if you do decide to go forward with your independent journey, you won't have finished the book until you sign. There's even a self-conducted signing ceremony waiting for you at the book's end.

In Stephen Covey's books and workshops, the personal effectiveness guru hammered home the concept of "principle-centered leadership." Think of my 13 covenants as principles to lead yourself by in your independent work. And remember that the biggest covenant of all isn't explicitly listed (though it encompasses the last four covenants): I will learn how to be good to myself while still demanding my best work. It's the hardest thing for many of us, but the most essential as an umbrella over all the other covenants. There are few things more tragic in the world of work than a brilliant, passionate, wildly creative, but needlessly burnt-out entrepreneur. Much more on avoiding independent burnout in Lesson 10.

## Getting Your Boss to Change

Your new boss now (that would be you if you've already made the leap) is permanent (unless you quit, which is not yet an option). Your boss isn't leaving or getting transferred or promoted or fired. So since s/he's not going anywhere, the only way you change your boss now—sorry to state the obvious—is to change yourself. You've no doubt had the experience of fantasizing about all the ways that your old bosses could have been different. You'll do the same thing with your new boss. Only this time it's a win-win. The first win is that you have some real control over getting this new boss to change. The second is that those changes will almost always be positive personal growth for you, and they will follow you everywhere. Even if someday you go back to work for someone else.

At first it didn't feel like a win-win for me. Not counting various pre-college adventures in entrepreneurship ranging from a calligraphy business at age 18 to fronting rock bands in college for weekend pocket money, I was 28 the first time I worked for myself as an adult. I had just left what had been a great job at a very successful San Francisco advertising agency. The agency was about to be acquired by a larger agency, and the word on the street was that things were going to get nasty for us, the acquirees. My boss there had actually been one of my best bosses, but a new Creative Director who was senior to me in the new pecking order had just come in. We'll call her Diana to protect the guilty.

Diana was very talented, but was also a very aggressive bull-in-a-china-shop personality. She was already making my life miserable in my role as account supervisor responsible for one of the agency's largest accounts. Her job was to create advertising; mine was to first develop the communication strategy and then help her sell her commercial or ad to the client. She was all about getting clients to buy her latest idea (without offering them alternative ideas as was customary at the time). Her take-it-or-leave-it approach annoyed me, and it annoyed the client. For days I thought about how I could get Diana to change. I mapped out an entirely rational appeal with some emotional embellishments about how she could be a big hero with this client who loved having choices when considering new ad campaigns. Then with some trepidation I finally marched into her office about a week before a crucial presentation that we were to jointly make to the client. There she was, leaning over a storyboard (the sequence of drawings depicting the camera shots for a commercial). Putting my best diplomatic foot forward, I said something like, "Diana, I'd like to talk with you about next week's presentation; no doubt you have it all under control but I've worked with this client for three years and I have some thoughts on how to help ensure that your great work gets sold." Decades later now, I still remember her reply verbatim. She spun around in her chair and looked at me with a scornful squint and said, "Your only job in that meeting will be to hold the client's mouth open wide enough for me to shove this storyboard down his throat!" I waited a second for her to laugh, but the laugh never came. So much for diplomacy.

I was already thinking about leaving the agency with a new regime coming in that seemed like a bad cultural fit for me, but this conversation with Diana was the moment my circuit breaker tripped. I decided one of us had to go. She certainly wasn't budging, and I didn't believe I could change her even if I was willing to try to change myself. I also didn't believe I could work with her (and *for* her, given her seniority). The silver lining, of course, was the beginning of a long career working independently. Belated thanks, Diana, for the big shove!

The point of this story is that, working for myself, I was soon struck by how often I wanted my new boss (me) to act differently. You may well find that changing yourself can be at least as challenging as getting a former boss to change. As Ben Franklin said (and Mick Jagger sang nearly 250 years later), "Old habits die hard," and some of those habits are almost always exacerbated when working independently. We've already covered pushing yourself. But then there's "Now that it's all me, everything has to be perfect because everything I do reflects my worth as a human being." Or how about "I'm working for myself now so I really do have to control everything." These are among the gnarliest examples from my own experience, and we'll explore them in detail in Lessons 5 and 6, respectively. The thing is, when you're working independently you will have to grow and change in ways you never did when you had a boss who isn't you. And pushing yourself to grow is very different than pushing yourself to overwork. Growth is harder, but it's a beautiful thing—spilling over into the other parts of your life to great benefit.

Before delving more deeply into these and all the other challenges of independent work, let's look more closely at why you would want to leave that paycheck behind in the first place. How sure *are* you?

\* \* \*

# LESSON 2

◆

# Know Your Motives (and Be Honest with Yourself!)

◆

*"Be honest with yourself, or life will never be honest with you."*
~ Leigh Brackett

*"We do not deal much in fact when we are contemplating ourselves."*
~ Mark Twain

If you haven't cut the cord yet and are still deciding, a good first question is this: *am I running toward something, or away from something*? There may have been some wildly successful self-employeds who were not passionate about their independent work, but I haven't met them yet. There is also the possibility that you don't care about being wildly successful, but would just like to do some quality work on your own that pays the bills and avoids some of the hassles of your previous or current job. Nothing wrong with that. That may be quite doable as long as you're talented enough, can sell what you do, and can find enough meaning for it to be reasonably satisfying. I don't want to set the bar too low, but it's not for me to pass judgment. Only to say that the more passion and vision, the greater the likelihood of rewards—financial as well as intangible.

## Looking Yourself in the Eye

So now it's time to get honest—real honest—and strip away everything that isn't the truth. Why do you want to work independently?

No, really—why? I'm forever amazed at how many people I've encountered who set off on this journey without clarity on this. It's a different issue than lack of clarity about your destination, or lack of a compass or adequate navigation plan. When 102 pilgrims set out for the new world from Plymouth, England in September 1620, there were at least two different answers as to why. For some, they were intent on finding a safe place to practice their religion. Others were entrepreneurs intent on finding better economic opportunities than those available at the time in England and The Netherlands. Though the pilgrims' compass proved no match for the storms that blew The Mayflower off course and landed it in Massachusetts instead of Virginia, everyone aboard was pretty darned clear on why they were on this voyage even if blown further north than planned. Their whys were still intact even if their where had shifted.

Some of us, however, when we make a change, knowing exactly where we're going—and initially even navigating perfectly to the destination—still haven't adequately explored the depths of why. Have you?

When I was 32, and four years into a successful independent consultancy called U.S. Marketing Services (nothing stopping you from trying to sound big when you're just starting out on your own!), I baffled friends and family by moving to Los Angeles to go back to school full-time to study music composition. (I admit to holding on to one long-term client throughout that experience to pay some bills.) The circumstances were too idiosyncratic to catalog here, but the essence was this: that as much as I enjoyed some early success in business, a desire to become literate in music—I couldn't read it, or accurately write down the music I heard in my head when I "wrote" songs—had been clawing at me for years. It was time to learn. In fact, I told myself that not only was I dying to write songs, but that that's what I wanted to do for a living. I would get the additional training I needed to do it right, and then I'd be on my way. Off to Hollywood I went. Within months I was knee-deep in music theory and composition classes, building a home recording studio (more challenging—and expensive—back in those days before technology radically democratized recording), and starting to make demo recordings of my songs.

At the core of all this, however, was an embarrassing truth highly relevant to independent work. Even now it's hard to publicly admit, and I've never said it out loud. In the rearview mirror I can see that at that time I was probably more interested in *being* a hit songwriter than in *writing* the songs. Yes, I found great pleasure in the writing, but if I was truly honest with myself I would have seen that my principal obsession then was becoming one of the top ten songwriters in the business, making money, and knowing that my music would be heard long after I was gone.

This element of ego-feeding grandiosity, in retrospect, was more focused on outcomes than on the actual act of writing. It seems shallow and immature now. But I was still young enough to be in a "go big or go home" state of mind, fixated on material success rooted in my lower-middle-class upbringing by two struggling working parents. And I was also an introvert. Unlike a rock star, I wanted to be able to walk down the street and have no one recognize me—maybe not even recognize my name—but with people hearing my songs pouring out of every speaker everywhere they went. And, yes, I wanted the royalties to be pouring in too. Ironically, all these years later, it's the writing of the songs (when I have time) that I'm authentically passionate about now, as I long ago released on writing "hits." In fact, what drove me away from the music business was an industry that increasingly demanded I write formula radio hits for teenagers instead of writing from my heart. Now I do write honest songs from the heart, and I'm sure they're my best creative work. Not commercial, so not much in royalties, but far more satisfying—and a great lesson in the importance of honesty in independent work. In fact, I strongly suspect now that I would have had greater success in Los Angeles had I written from heart at the outset despite what the market told me it wanted.

The point of this story is the importance of separating ego from meaning and passion. Authenticity can take you far in independent work, as in life. So when you deeply confront whether you're running away from something (which may or may not include a horrible boss or soul-sucking work) or running *toward* something, get very clear on what it is that you're running toward. And especially *why*. Hopefully it's much more specific than just running toward the *idea* of working independently. Loving the hour-to-hour challenges of entrepreneurship or the great feeling of satisfaction in creating something new and useful are very different things than loving the idea of being an entrepreneur or your own boss. Or even the idea of being a free spirit.

## Getting to the Truth

Whether or not you have children, try the exercise of being a 5-year-old again. 5-year-olds are experts at asking why. Persistently. My daughter taught me that many years ago.

"Why is the sky blue, Daddy?"

"Well, the light coming from the sun is made up of all the colors in a rainbow, Sweetie, but on clear days the blue light is scattered throughout the air more than the other colors."

"Why, Daddy?"

"Because light travels in waves [I gesture with a wavy hand]—you can't see the waves, only the colors—and the waves of some colors scatter more easily than other colors. Blue is the color that scatters easiest." (She was really smart but only 5—what was I thinking?)

"Why, Daddy?"

"Because blue waves are smaller than any other color's waves."

"Why, Daddy?"

At this point the conversation is clearly getting so far above my pay grade that I'm just digging myself a deeper hole. (Apologies in arrears to my kid, now a very successful high school teacher despite these early rambling punishments from a science-loving father.) However, pursuing the *why* line of questioning in this fashion pays great dividends when getting to the real truth of why you want to work independently. So, at least take a quiet, focused hour and be a 5-year-old. And go for the throat with "why?". After that, if you're not truly convinced that you've gotten to the very bottom of this, rinse and repeat as needed until you are. In Lesson 4 you'll be called upon to articulate your truth.

## Past Performance is No Guarantee of Future Results

If you happen to be an investor, you've likely run across the standard disclaimer attached to mutual funds, ETF's (exchange-traded funds), and other investment instruments: "Past performance is no guarantee of future results." The same certainly applies to work. But maybe not the way you think. Yes, the obvious meaning in that context is just because you were able to get good results as part of a team or larger organization doesn't mean that you will get them on your own. But there's a bigger issue here, especially if you're in the first half of your career.

When you're really unhappy in your job, and you haven't had that many jobs, there's a tendency to assume that most companies are just hard to work for if you happen to be you. That can push you toward independent work as an escape, and running away is something we've already identified as a weak case for success. In the preface of this book I said that there would be multiple times when I would raise the question of whether you're really cut out for working independently. Part of getting to the truth is having some modicum of objectivity in appraising what it is you're leaving behind. There is so much to be said for steady and predictable income, for a more structured day, for friendships among colleagues, and for the shared satisfactions of teamwork. Just because you've had an unsatisfactory experience so far at Company X and even at Company Y and possibly even at Company Z doesn't mean there aren't a lot more companies that are great places to work and just haven't found you yet. So be careful not to project forward too much based on experience to date.

My last job in a big company so many years ago was, quite honestly, brutal. It was a vice president position that was scoped too big for any mortal, and after I resigned it was (of course!) split into two jobs. This was a huge, regimented, century-old company with an inflexible top-down management culture. (One of my bosses was a wonderful person but his previous executive job was military: a general in the Pentagon. Really. Few things make one feel more subordinate than reporting to a military general.) I had never before held an executive position in a company that large; I quit after working there for three years, and soon realized I had subconsciously extrapolated from this experience that most other big companies wouldn't be that different. So I turned down some very good executive-level opportunities at other companies during those following months.

The silver lining was that, once again, I ended up with my freedom. But believe me, there have been many times during some financially "softer" years of working independently when I've wondered if I couldn't have happily thrived inside other companies while also enjoying the stability, the health insurance, the 401K matching, etc. This is all another way of saying that, when you ask yourself if you're running away from something, make sure it isn't a particular dysfunction of your current employer that is not widely generalizable to other companies. Otherwise you may end up as a last-resort "reluctant entrepreneur" who has prematurely decided that working for a company—any company—is not for you. Then you've unnecessarily limited your options for livelihood and fulfillment.

But for now, let's assume that you're seeking independence for the right reasons and running toward something that is right for you.

## Truth Can Be a Moving Target

As you move through the rest of this book, and then through an independent career if that's the route you choose, remember that today's truth can be tomorrow's deception. We grow, we change, the world changes, and we can certainly outgrow yesteryear's truths.

So it's important to think of your truth as a movie and not a photograph fixed in time. That means ongoing reevaluation of *why*, at frequent enough intervals to head off divergence between your *current* truth and what you're doing in your independent work. My songwriting story was an example of how my truth shifted over the years, as *why* shifted from outer success to inner fulfillment and self-expression. We'll discuss tracking the truth in Lesson 8 so that you're more likely to see change coming and can react productively.

But to get to the bottom of your current truth, let's say that you've now had your inner 5-year-old interrogate you, maybe even multiple times—whatever it took—and you're convinced that independent work is for you. And now you know *why*, because you've committed it to writing. (Covenant 2 refresher for you and your new boss: *We will both be very clear on the reasons why I want to work independently or start a new business, and I will thoughtfully and honestly commit those reasons to writing—in priority order of importance, and before we commence.*) If you haven't yet done that, there's no time like the present to lay down this book and grab a pen, pencil, keyboard, or voice recorder. This will also help prepare you for Lesson 3.

## That Takes Care of Why, But What About the What?

With *why* in tow, some of you lucky ones know exactly what it is that you want to do independently. Others will think you know, but will find out sooner or later that you actually didn't. And still others will already know that you don't know. (You have the desire to break out, but without a clear vision or plan.) For all of you except the very most certain among the very most certain, that brings us to the art—and science—of making good choices.

\* \* \*

# LESSON 3

◆

# Make a Disciplined Choice Among the Many Paths to Independence

◆

*"Choices are the hinges of destiny."*
~ Edwin Markham

*"Ever notice that 'What the hell' is always the right decision?"*
~ Marilyn Monroe

Not always, Marilyn. Many self-employment failures come not from lack of effort or smarts, but from lack of discipline in initially identifying one's needs and what will meet them. Half the battle in getting what you want is avoiding side streets that have you chasing something you think you want, only to find out that it's far less satisfying than you expected. Not everyone is able to enjoy what they asked for when they finally get it. (Like Willie Nelson joked, a skeleton walks into a bar and says to the bartender, "Gimme a beer—and a mop.")

Unless you're just a skeleton, few decisions are as emotionally charged as choosing how you're going to spend the majority of your waking hours. But when it comes to this thing called "work," even the most abstract of considerations can be looked at with more rationality and discipline than you may think. Unless you're dead certain of exactly what you want to do, and that it's tightly aligned with your needs, values, priorities, and truth, you will want to evaluate alternatives as methodically as possible. And for some of you, one of those alternatives may be not working independently at all. But we'll come to that later in this chapter.

## Clarifying Your Needs, and What Will Meet Them

When we evaluate any set of alternatives, we need two things before we can start: (1) alternatives that are well enough defined to know what we're evaluating, and (2) a set of well-defined criteria on which to evaluate them. The pitfalls when trying to get those two things right have revealed themselves over and over in choices made by client companies I've advised over the years. As I've also seen with my coaching clients, those pitfalls are at least as relevant to us as individuals when choosing the path forward for independent work (or, for that matter, for remaining employed).

In business, strategy is all about making choices, and executives and consultants invest much time and money in analyzing those choices. So in charting your personal path, what can we learn from how disciplined, market-leading companies formulate strategy? Or, for a more concrete example, what can we learn from how they optimize choices when deciding what new product innovations to invest in? Many millions, sometimes billions, of dollars/euros/yuan/yen are at stake in revenue and costs. (Yes, I know—your personal fate is worth more than that! Priceless, in fact.)

When I advise client companies on what new products to make (and not make), and what features and functions those products should have (and not have), I approach that with a patented methodology called Strategic Harmony® that has also been adapted for personal coaching and career coaching. What can we take away from the fact that many more new products fail in the marketplace than succeed? Time and again I've found that the majority of product failures can be traced back to one of two causes that precede any mistakes in product design, manufacturing, or pricing. The first is that the company evaluated those products on the wrong criteria, or on criteria that were inadequately defined or poorly prioritized. The second cause is that the definition of the product at the outset was too vague. The result was that each person on the evaluation team either had a different vision of what the product would be, or didn't understand it clearly enough to really know what they were evaluating.

So what about you? Whether you're choosing between two or among a handful of alternative scenarios for independent work, or just choosing between one independent scenario and staying at your current company, the same principles apply.

Let's look at your criteria before delving into your alternative paths. I start with the criteria because you'll want the evaluation of those alternatives to be guided by the criteria that are most important to your fulfillment, effectiveness, and ultimate success. I call these criteria *drivers of satisfaction*. Satisfaction with work is a mashup of happiness, purpose, and self-actualization that brings an ongoing sense of meaningfulness and well-being. Independent work or otherwise, purpose-driven work will always be both easier and more satisfying than just working to earn a buck. It matters little whether you call your criteria drivers of satisfaction, drivers of meaning, drivers of joy, or drivers of inner peace. What matters is that you're very clear on what defines your ideal work experience, so that the path you choose—though it will always have trade-offs and can never optimize all your criteria—can land you in the best possible place.

## Adapting Maslow: Your Hierarchy of Work Needs

For those of you not familiar with Maslow's "Hierarchy of Needs," Abraham Maslow, the influential 20th-century psychologist, forged groundbreaking theories regarding motivation, personality, and human behavior. His Hierarchy of Needs framework was visually expressed as a pyramid with the most basic human needs for survival (such as food, water, warmth, sleep) at the bottom foundational layer, and "self-actualization" needs at the top (such as creativity and problem-solving). In between were safety needs, the need for love and belonging, and esteem-related needs such as respect and feelings of accomplishment.

In evaluating your options for work or career, you will have a more tightly scoped hierarchy of needs that's a subset of Maslow's hierarchy. But there are two highly relevant things about Maslow's hierarchy that can help you more accurately predict not only whether independent work is really for you but also what that work should (and shouldn't) be. The first is simply the fact that needs are indeed a hierarchy—a set of desires that are not all equal in importance. So when defining your drivers of satisfaction—what you need from your work—the importance of thoughtfully ranking those needs is implied.

Secondly, since the role work plays in your life comprises abstract intangible needs as well as tangible ones like money, it's crucial to do all you can to define those abstract needs in terms that are as concrete as possible. What good is thoughtfully prioritizing needs if those needs are poorly defined?

Let's delve into both of these requirements to help you get to a hierarchy of *your* drivers of satisfaction that can most productively serve as evaluation criteria for different work options that you may wish to explore.

### Identifying and Defining Work-Related Drivers of Satisfaction

When you really take some quality time to think about and write down what's important to you in your world of work, you'll inevitably produce a tapestry of positives and negatives—positives you'll want to accentuate and negatives you'll want to mitigate or avoid altogether with your choice of work. Springboards for honing in on positive needs include identifying the experiences and circumstances that have made you feel:

- Happiest
- Most stimulated
- Proudest
- Most fulfilled
- Most authentic
- Making the most of your talents/skills
- Most helpful to others

Springboards for identifying negatives to mitigate or avoid include reflecting on what episodes, circumstances, or even people have ever made you feel:

- Anxious
- Diminished
- Insecure
- Annoyed
- Overwhelmed
- Under-utilized
- Undervalued
- Or especially the inverse of your "positives" above (e.g., unhappy, unfulfilled, inauthentic, etc.)

There will typically be somewhere between five and ten criteria that really matter to you when evaluating work options. Any beyond that are likely to be subsets of, or sub-points that further define, those five to ten. Or they will be "noise"—inconsequential in the overall scheme of things, so we want to exclude those for the sake of clarity and focus.

A coaching client of mine who we'll call Richard, in his early 50's and ready to make a change, thoughtfully went through the springboards exercise and produced the following criteria (not necessarily in this order; we'll discuss prioritization shortly) for evaluating work options:

- Aligns with my values
- Highly leverages my talent and experience
- Highly valued by clients/customers
- Provides financial security
- Enables healthy work-life balance
- Gives me more control
- Reasonable odds for success
- Allows me to work past retirement age

Richard is now ready to evaluate his options on these criteria, right? Wrong. Not yet. His criteria set is just fine at the high level, but some of these abstractions need much more granular definitions.

I have a three-word mantra that addresses *sequence* when getting your drivers of satisfaction into sharp focus: **Identify > Define > Prioritize**. "Identify" and "define" may sound like the same thing. They aren't. Most work-related needs, other than money and certain benefits, are more abstract than they are concrete. Once an abstract need has been identified, it needs to be defined in a more concrete way to facilitate thoughtful evaluation of alternatives on that need.

For example, "Aligns with my values" might be one of your identified needs as it was for Richard. If so, what *are* your values? Articulate them. Whether it's helping people, protecting the environment, taking care of your family, or making lots of money—whatever those things are, be honest. This is not about judging yourself; it's about zeroing in on what's authentically important to you. This is not an exercise to be taken lightly. Intangible values are full of loaded words.

As another example, it's easy to confuse *happiness* and *meaningfulness* if you don't unpack them as best you can to deeply understand what each of those concepts are to you and what expectations you have from them. For some, meaningfulness of work is about improving a particular group of people's lives. For some it's the thrill of doing something very well that they thought they might never be able to do. For some it's about creating a legacy that does some good in the world even after they stop working. For others, it's work that by its nature has profound moments that aren't really happy at all, like a hospice worker who eases the passing of the terminally ill, or a grief counselor who helps people go deep into their sorrow and ease their transit to where the light is. You may find, as distinguished psychologist James Hollis suggests, that meaningfulness outweighs happiness—that meaningful moments are, as Hollis puts it, "more moving engagements with others, with mystery, with curiosity and its discoveries, than anything the world names happiness. ... Happiness is transient, but meaning abides."

In whatever way you wrestle with needs like meaningfulness or happiness, you can't evaluate anything on such criteria without first making these abstractions as specific as possible. What are their component parts? (For *you*, as each definition is individual.) How do you know them when you see or feel them? What do they do to your senses?

Let's look at another of Richard's needs: "More control." Control over *what* exactly? Control over how he works? Over when he works? Over who he collaborates with? Over what's expected of him? You can see the difference between just identifying a need and defining what you've identified.

When making career decisions, there's no getting around a lot of touchy-feely abstractions. But I've never seen an abstraction that can't be at least somewhat concretized. Earlier I mentioned the Strategic Harmony® method for evaluating companies' alternative investments in innovation, and what we can learn from that approach in personal decision-making. When companies are making products for customers, customer needs—just like your work-related needs—are both tangible and intangible. When, for example, you buy a portable wireless audio speaker to stream music, you likely care about tangibles like price and speaker size. But you may be even more focused on subjective factors: you want that speaker to sound great, be easy to use, and have a cool design. That doesn't tell engineers and designers what to build unless they know what customers think "great" sound is, what "easy" really means to them, and how they define "cool."

I reiterate: just because these needs are abstractions doesn't mean they don't have discrete component parts. In the context of portable speakers, "great sound" may mean measurable metrics like clarity of vocals and instruments, deep bass, no hum or noise, and can play loud enough without distortion. "Easy" may mean easy to initially set up (simple instructions, all necessary hardware included, easy to connect my smartphone, etc.) and easy to use (intuitive controls, bug-free software, long battery life). I think you're getting the hang of it. Granted, even for these speakers, some of the more specific attributes are more concrete and more easily measured (like battery life) than others (like intuitive controls). But they are all subsets of the higher-level 'parent' attributes (great sound, easy, etc.), helping to define abstractions in a more concrete way. And the more concrete the definition of your work-related needs—your drivers of satisfaction as criteria for evaluating alternatives—the more disciplined and productive your decision-making will be.

## The 5-Year-Old Strikes Again

This is where the 5-year-old can again be pressed into service. Only this time it's *what* instead of why. What *really* matters. When you identify an abstract need like "work-life balance," enlist your inner 5-year-old again to put more concrete color on that.

"What does work-life balance mean, Mommy?"

"Well, it means having enough time to do the things I want to do besides my work."

"What things, Mommy?"

"Things like spending time with you, or going hiking in the woods with you and Daddy, or taking family vacations in faraway places, or making our house pretty, or working in the garden, or even having some of the alone time that all mommies need."

"Why do you need alone time, Mommy?"

We won't answer that here (where we have the luxury of ducking the tougher questions like "Why wouldn't you rather spend that alone time with me, Mommy?"), but you can see that now we're getting somewhere with making abstractions more concrete and putting a finer point on what's really important. That inner 5-year-old has just gotten this mommy closer to being able to judge how many working hours a week might be realistic while still allowing time for the "life" part of work-life balance. Then, in turn, it becomes easier for her to evaluate alternative scenarios for work, self-employed or otherwise, on this criterion. (Just to be clear, despite this example, let me assure you that I never want to have to truly separate "life" and "work." Whether or not you're your own boss, doing the work that's right for you will blur that line, as the joys of work and the other parts of your life feed each other.)

### Relative Importance of Needs: Prioritization

Now that we've identified and defined needs, we can prioritize those drivers of satisfaction with a better sense of what it is we're prioritizing. (Remember: Identify>Define>Prioritize.) A coaching client we'll call Angela was a successful sales manager for a well-known technology company. She loved sales, but she felt the pull of being more in control and had been restless for some time—though there was much to like about her company. She was trying to decide between four alternatives: staying with her current employer, taking a sales job at another company, starting an online business with her best friend, or joining a network of sales training professionals that would allow her to work independently as a trainer and be her own boss. She identified seven distinct drivers of satisfaction that collectively defined fulfillment for her. She methodically evaluated her four alternatives on each of those seven criteria. When the criteria were weighted equally, staying with her current employer outscored the other alternatives, appearing to be the best fit. It actually had a moderately strong score on six of her seven criteria. Though it looked like the "winner," that was *before* prioritization of criteria was factored in. When she went through a considered process of weighting those criteria in importance, allocating 100 "salience points" across the seven needs, the array looked like this:

| Criterion | Salience (as percent of total criteria) |
|---|---|
| Need "D" | 35% |
| Need "B" | 20% |
| Need "G" | 15% |
| Need "A" | 10% |
| Need "E" | 10% |
| Need "C" | 5% |
| Need "F" | 5% |
| TOTAL | 100% of Angela's most significant needs |

In other words, even though all seven needs were important to Angela, Need "D" turned out to be seven times more salient than Needs "C" or "F". (Let's say "about" seven times, as this type of exercise is at least as qualitative as it is quantitative.) Again, the overarching point here is that all needs are not equal and their differences must be accounted for in decision-making. When the scores for each of her work alternatives were then modified by the relative importance of each criterion, joining the network of sales trainers showed itself as an even better fit than staying in her current job. That's because, even though sales training had mediocre scores on three of the criteria, it scored well on the three that were most important—high on "B" and very high on "D" and "G".

I realize this all sounds quite clinical for an exercise as emotional as making career choices. But there is plenty of emotion in identifying and defining what these drivers of satisfaction actually are for you. You'll want a healthy blend of emotion and rationality in the first two parts of *Identify > Define > Prioritize*, but prioritization by its nature is best served by translating your subjective instincts and thoughtfulness into some approximation of quantitative outputs. That's where the salience points come in.

So now that we've talked about how to choose among choices, let's talk about what those choices are. What are your alternative paths? And which one best serves your authentic self?

The many paths to independent work can be overwhelming to sort through. There are more varied opportunities than ever as the incidence of independent work continues to rise, and as more of us have had the experience through the Covid-19 pandemic of working from home with technology-enabled tools. The emerging gig economy creates yet more hybrid possibilities as well. Especially if you're multi-talented and have lots of interests, the range of options can be as daunting as it is exciting. But even if you're just choosing between what you're doing now and one other possibility, a disciplined evaluation on drivers of satisfaction is just as important as when choosing among a basket of multiple alternatives.

## Include Your Current Job (if you have one) in Any Evaluation

There's a reason that "You don't know what you've got till it's gone" is a cliché. It's obviously important to know in advance as much as possible about whether that greener grass on the other side is actually greener or less green than the grass you're in now. I notice that sometimes when clients are comparing alternatives, they forget to include the one they're living right now as a benchmark. Yet it's likely the one that you know the most about at this moment.

Sometimes as employees we've forgotten how we got to where we are—why we took this job in the first place, and why we were so excited about it (assuming it wasn't only for the money, which is usually a bad idea). Unless you're absolutely sure that it's time to move on, the process of thoughtfully scoring your current job in any evaluation of alternatives can sometimes reconnect you with reasons why you may not really want to leave it. Or it could just confirm that your instincts about it being time for a change are spot on. Either way, there is value in not overlooking the present when deciding about the future.

### Inductive Reasoning Pays Off

With your drivers of satisfaction identified, defined, and prioritized, and a clear articulation of alternative paths, you now have the tools you need for making a disciplined choice. At every intersection of each path with each driver—that is, how would each path likely impact each of your needs, positively or negatively—your judgment in scoring those intersections will produce the building blocks for a sounder decision. So by the time you have scored, say, three different paths and your current situation against, say, seven prioritized needs, you've produced 28 building blocks weighted by the relative importance of each need. At that point you have inductively built a choice on a foundation of 28 separate and thoughtfully considered decisions, based on the right questions, and preceded by thoughtful ranking of the relative importance of your criteria. You have not only rationalized a choice, but also baked in emotional and psychological considerations.

So, ready to take the plunge? Not so fast. Especially if this will be your first plunge into independent work, a final and crucial safety check is in order. You may have clearly identified what you want and a path to get it, but are you suited to the journey's demands? That brings us to Lesson 4.

\* \* \*

# LESSON 4

◆

# Confront Who You Really Are Before Taking the Plunge

◆

*"Before you find out who you are, you have to figure out who you aren't."*
~ Iyanla Vanzant

*"The ingenuity of self-deception is inexhaustible."*
~ Hannah More

*Know thyself.* Those words (ΓΝΩΘΙ ΣΑΥΤΟΝ, actually) were inscribed on the Greek Temple of Apollo at Delphi more than 2300 years ago, and have been echoed through the ages from Socrates on down. Nothing is more important when considering independent work. Ruthless introspection is a key ingredient in the recipe for successful self-employment, despite the old quip about how the time you might waste knowing thyself could otherwise be used to make more desirable acquaintances.

I like to assume that all my readers are desirable acquaintances, and I want to ensure that the desires of those desirable acquaintances can be fulfilled by independent work—if that's what your heart desires. Better to know sooner than later if your heart's desire may turn out to be an ugly case of "be careful what you wish for."

You might wonder why I didn't start with this chapter. After all, why read any further than the topic of whether independent work is a good fit for you if it isn't? Well, I remember learning a lot about myself when testing the assumptions we've tested in the opening chapters, and confronting more fully what it means to make disciplined choices. So I thought in previous chapters you too might learn some things about yourself that would better prepare you for this one.

Accordingly, here we step back to ask the larger question of whether you're really cut out for independent work. If you're already sufficiently confident about that (or already well on your way in your independent journey), by all means feel free to skip ahead to Part II: Making It Happen. But even people who fall madly in love and know that their significant other is Mr. or Ms. Right, they still can get a bad case of nerves on the eve of their wedding. So if you're not really *really* sure, I invite you to take the following quiz.

## A Final Check-In Before Taking the Plunge: The No Boss Quiz

The No Boss Quiz is, granted, a misnomer, as I've already called attention to the fact that when you step out on your own you'll be bossing yourself around. But independent work is the closest you'll get to having no boss—short of unemployment (the ultimate No Boss strategy, though seldom recommended without pre-existing independent wealth).

---

The quiz: There are 30 "questions" (in the form of statements) below. You're being asked to decide to what degree you agree or disagree with each statement as it pertains to you personally. Answer honestly and thoughtfully, taking all the time you need. (Did I mention *honestly*? This is *not* something you want to fudge, lest you be cast into an environment likely to be hostile to you. Besides, it's embarrassment-proof: your responses are private unless you show them to someone.)

*For each statement, circle the number from 1 to 5 that best describes your attitudes, beliefs, and behaviors.*

***1 = Strongly Disagree, 2 = Disagree, 3 = Neither Agree nor Disagree, 4 = Agree, 5 = Strongly Agree.***

*If you find any statement truly irrelevant to your circumstances, circle "N/A" (not applicable). But strive to answer at least 25 of the 30 statements with a numeric response.*

| | | | | | | |
|---|---|---|---|---|---|---|
| 1. I don't feel like I can be my authentic self at work. | 1 | 2 | 3 | 4 | 5 | N/A |
| 2. I have above-average tolerance for uncertainty. | 1 | 2 | 3 | 4 | 5 | N/A |
| 3. I have a deep understanding of my strengths and weaknesses. | 1 | 2 | 3 | 4 | 5 | N/A |
| 4. I think persistence is as important as talent or capability. | 1 | 2 | 3 | 4 | 5 | N/A |
| 5. Asking for help from others is rarely a sign of weakness. | 1 | 2 | 3 | 4 | 5 | N/A |
| 6. I am bothered but never panic when things at work aren't going well. | 1 | 2 | 3 | 4 | 5 | N/A |
| 7. I know what it feels like to not have a paycheck. | 1 | 2 | 3 | 4 | 5 | N/A |
| 8. For my age, I'm comfortable with my level and pace of retirement savings. | 1 | 2 | 3 | 4 | 5 | N/A |
| 9. When investing in the stock market, I think less about the risk than the reward. | 1 | 2 | 3 | 4 | 5 | N/A |

| | | | | | | |
|---|---|---|---|---|---|---|
| 10. If I had to go at least one year with no income while also having a modest increase in expenses, that would be financially manageable. | 1 | 2 | 3 | 4 | 5 | N/A |
| 11. If I had to go at least one year with no income while also having an increase in expenses, that would be emotionally and psychologically manageable. | 1 | 2 | 3 | 4 | 5 | N/A |
| 12. I'm good at setting boundaries with my family and friends. | 1 | 2 | 3 | 4 | 5 | N/A |
| 13. I'm good at setting boundaries with my boss. | 1 | 2 | 3 | 4 | 5 | N/A |
| 14. I'm a good judge of people and character. | 1 | 2 | 3 | 4 | 5 | N/A |
| 15. I am more of an introvert than an extrovert. | 1 | 2 | 3 | 4 | 5 | N/A |
| 16. I have no trouble letting go of an idea if it doesn't seem to be resonating with other people. | 1 | 2 | 3 | 4 | 5 | N/A |

| | | | | | | |
|---|---|---|---|---|---|---|
| 17. I would be okay with not having opportunities to bounce ideas off other people in my workplace. | 1 | 2 | 3 | 4 | 5 | N/A |
| 18. I doubt I would be much affected by missing the camaraderie and social aspects of seeing co-workers at my workplace most days. | 1 | 2 | 3 | 4 | 5 | N/A |
| 19. During the workday, I spend very little time on social media or the internet that is not related to my work. | 1 | 2 | 3 | 4 | 5 | N/A |
| 20. When I see errors in my work, they sometimes bother me but I don't obsess about them. | 1 | 2 | 3 | 4 | 5 | N/A |
| 21. More of the structure and goal-setting in my work life is provided by me than by my boss or company. | 1 | 2 | 3 | 4 | 5 | N/A |
| 22. I have resented more than I've appreciated most of my bosses. | 1 | 2 | 3 | 4 | 5 | N/A |
| 23. While employed during Covid, I loved working from home. | 1 | 2 | 3 | 4 | 5 | N/A |

| | | | | | | |
|---|---|---|---|---|---|---|
| 24. If I had to work from home most of the time, I could keep distractions to a minimum. | 1 | 2 | 3 | 4 | 5 | N/A |
| 25. I do a pretty good job of taking care of myself to ensure physical and mental well-being. | 1 | 2 | 3 | 4 | 5 | N/A |
| 26. I need more flexibility regarding when I take my time off from work. | 1 | 2 | 3 | 4 | 5 | N/A |
| 27. If I no longer had paid vacation time, I would feel fine about taking at least as much vacation as I've been allowed in my last job. | 1 | 2 | 3 | 4 | 5 | N/A |
| 28. I pay attention to when I'm overworking to the detriment of my health. | 1 | 2 | 3 | 4 | 5 | N/A |
| 29. I generally handle stress very well. | 1 | 2 | 3 | 4 | 5 | N/A |
| 30. When I imagine working for myself, I picture success. | 1 | 2 | 3 | 4 | 5 | N/A |

Now, take a moment. Stretch. Breathe. Then do the following:

1. Look over your responses and be sure you're comfortable that they are as honest and accurate as possible.
2. Change them if indicated by second thoughts.
3. When satisfied, add up your points from all responses.
4. Divide the total points by the total number of statements you scored on the 1-to-5 scale (i.e., omitting all N/A's). For example, if you responded N/A to five statements (and it shouldn't be more than five), divide your total points by 25 (30 statements minus 5).
5. The result is your score. Before I provide context for your score, read the important disclosure below.

*Disclaimer:* *I am neither a psychologist nor a survey research expert. The latter would make this more scientific and methodologically sophisticated, with more nuanced approaches to statement sequence, wording, and weighting of scores. I know this because, in my own career, I have on behalf of my clients worked with some of the world's most highly regarded firms that specialize in survey research. But I offer this quiz unapologetically as at least one modest and imprecise step toward quantifying suitability for independent work, based on subjective considerations other than your intelligence and skills. While scholars and research designers have survey and measurement expertise superior to my own, few of them have my 30-plus years of independent work experience to bake into this. The statements in the quiz are not derived from empirical quantitative research or psychological profiling, but rather from decades of observing myself and the many successful (and unsuccessful) self-employeds that I've known over the years. These statements reflect traits and beliefs that provide both headwinds and tailwinds for independent work—what has helped or hurt the No Boss experience and its results, and what has constrained me or propelled me forward.*

**So please take away this ABOVE ALL: your score is far less important than the fact that you've now reflected on the statements**

*in the quiz.* That action, regardless of score, and as complement to the rest of this book, will deepen your ability to anticipate how well you'll perform and how satisfied you'll be when self-employed—and whether long-term independent work will, for you, be paradise or purgatory.

## Context for Your Score

Notice that I called this a quiz rather than a survey. *Survey* connotes professionally-designed research that stands up to time-honored standards and protocols. Professionally-designed surveys take great pains to minimize response bias. That includes wording questions or statements in ways such that the respondent doesn't know that answering a certain way will produce a predictable outcome. Yet it was likely obvious before you were even one quarter of the way through this quiz that, the more you agreed with these statements, the better suited you likely are for independent work.

There were methods to my madness in designing it this way, not least of which is that the statements in the quiz provide a nice reference checklist to continue reflecting upon as you make what may be a life-changing decision to become your own boss. But it also makes it somewhat easier to provide context, if oversimplified, for your score.

Generally, an overall score of 4.0 or higher is a very promising indicator that you're a good fit for independent work. It means that you somewhat or strongly agree with most of these statements that profile successful self-employeds. Of course that is no guarantee of success, especially if you don't have a compelling idea, product, or service, as well as some good business sense and access to sufficient resources to get started.

However, a lower score shouldn't necessarily dissuade you. Just a couple of 1's or 2's on the scale that I used in the quiz can quickly drag your average down. Had I taken this same quiz when quitting my last job so many years ago, my best judgment now retrospectively is that my overall score would have been 3.8—even with a lot of

5's but because of just a few 2's. Again, the value here is less about the score, and much more about seriously pondering these statements, looking at any that you may have scored with a 1, 2, or even 3, and thinking about two things: (1) how those beliefs or behaviors are likely to impact your independent work and outcomes, and (2) what you can do to change those beliefs or behaviors—hard as that may be—that might raise those scores as you work on those things.

Working independently is like athletics. It requires not just dedication and persistence but also training the mind to think and behave in ways that make self-employment work for you. The themes you saw across the quiz statements—risk tolerance, uncertainty tolerance, financial security, work structure and goals, interaction with others (or lack thereof), personal boundaries—are all issues you want to pay special attention to with deep introspection in any decision regarding working for yourself. The stronger your coping strategies on these themes, the more fun and profit you're likely to experience when bossing yourself around.

## So Now What?

Just as we are all different, we all have a different relationship with our work. For some really passionate people doing what they love, the difference between work and play can be almost indistinguishable. For others, even among the world's most successful, not so much. (Elon Musk: "Being an entrepreneur is like eating glass and staring into the abyss of death." Muhammad Ali on boxing: "It's just a job. Grass grows, birds fly, waves pound the sand. I beat people up.") But I like to think that Confucius had it right when he wrote that if you choose work you love, you will never have to work a day in your life.

Finding such work is possible at great companies or independently. So now you have reached the seminal crossroads in this book. You're ready to decide, if you haven't already, that independent work is the best choice in serving your authentic self, or it isn't.

If it isn't, thanks for staying with me this long. I hope I've helped you find your truth. But if it is, or if you're at least leaning that way, let's get on to making it happen!

* * *

# PART II

♦

## Making It Happen

# LESSON 5

◆

# See Perfectionism for the Curse That It Is

◆

*"Il meglio è nemico del bene."*
*("Perfect is the enemy of good," loosely translated)*
~ Orlando Pescetti
(Italian Proverbs, 1603)


*"If I waited for perfection, I would never write a word."*
~ Margaret Atwood


This chapter title might cause you to suspect that I'm down on perfectionism. Not so. Just as our bodies have both beneficial bacteria and destructive bacteria, perfectionism can be extremely useful in many situations. Aviation, brain surgery, suspension bridge engineering, mission-critical software, auditable accounting, and Olympic gymnastics come to mind. But writing a relatively routine email to a client or customer is none of those things. The point of diminishing returns comes much sooner. So I'm all for dazzling my clients and having my home office humming with precision. It's just about knowing when enough is enough, and the stakes can be considerably higher when working independently where constraints on your time must mostly be self-imposed. I haven't seen a clinical study on the correlation between the entrepreneurial energy of people who choose to be their own boss and their incidence in high school of crying over a B+, but I suspect it's higher than for the population at large.

In total transparency, I reluctantly confess to scoring 92%—that's 30% above average—in Self-Oriented Perfectionism on the

Hewitt & Flett (psychologists) Multidimensional Perfectionism Test. Had there been Perfectionists Anonymous meetings in my city, I most certainly should have gone. It took me years to be self-aware enough to stand in front of a mirror and be able to say out loud, "My name is Steven Cristol, and I am a perfectionist." But self-employment certainly accelerated that process, because few things bring out the extremes of perfectionist tendencies as fast or as fiercely as working independently. When something you do is flawed, there is only one throat to choke—yours. And anyone who sees that flaw *knows* it's yours if they also know you're working alone. So now it reflects on you personally as well as professionally. And that ups the ante for "perfect."

But fear not, for consciousness is at hand. We start by revisiting Covenant 5: *We will diligently monitor the presence of perfectionism that is out of proportion to the task at hand, call it out when we see it, and adjust behavior accordingly.*

Let's parse this, starting with *"perfectionism that is out of proportion to the task at hand."* There's a place for perfectionism in crucial things even if you're not a brain surgeon or Olympic gymnast, whether it's getting an important client proposal just right or ensuring that invoices are accurate. The problem is that for most independent workers only a relatively small subset of what will fill your workdays is actually crucial. (Not radically different from your old job in that respect?) The rest comprises the "out of proportion" part. So think of perfectionism as a throttle: push it when truly justified, pull it back when it isn't. You likely should be pulling it much more often than pushing it if you're not a tax CPA on the eve of tax-filing day. It's taken me 30 years to fully understand that what makes self-employment sustainable is running it like a marathon instead of a 4-minute mile. And the tendency to sprint is much greater when you're not drawing a steady paycheck every couple of weeks.

I'm about to describe some sub-optimal self-employed behavior. Don't be insulted. There is nothing here that I haven't done myself, painful as it may be to disclose. And that brings us to *"diligently monitor"* in Covenant 5. If grasping the extent of my perfectionism took me far too long, it's because it's one thing to know about perfectionist tendencies but quite another to consistently notice when you're acting them out. Especially if you're acting them out multiple times a day, every day. This is where proactive self-surveillance comes in. You can't call out perfectionism and adjust behavior if you don't see it when it's happening. My "Perfectionism Audit" will help.

## The Perfectionism Audit

Perfectionism has much in common with other diseases; it has visible symptoms if you know where to look. But you also have to *remember* to look—to put your attention on certain aspects of work behavior that tend to escape our notice. The Perfectionism Audit has two pillars: symptoms and attention triggers (triggering you to notice when you may be perfecting unnecessarily). After the audit, we'll talk about mitigation and cures. But let's start with symptoms and attention so you'll know what you're looking for and really have your radar working. The following three symptoms are hallmarks of perfectionism for which working independently is a great temptress.

*Symptom #1: Things are taking too long.* The mother of all symptoms. The correlation between time and perfectionism is, well, almost perfect—especially in independent work. Perfectionism is rarely the shortest distance between two points. Ask Michelangelo (another independent worker, though not without apprentices). Fortunately, every email you will send or presentation you will make will likely not need to be the ceiling of the Sistine Chapel. That's why you'll want to look for three red flags that can help you spot perfectionism in the making when it's out of proportion to the task at hand. One flag occurs before the task, another during the task, and the third after the task.

Before a task, you find yourself worrying that you don't have enough time to do it the way you want to do it. That's a flag. Then during a task, be alert to that voice inside you that whispers much more often than it shouts, "This is taking too long." It's usually right; trust that inner wisdom. That's a flag. Then there's getting to the end of your day and wondering why you only accomplished a fraction of what you thought you would or could. Another flag. Especially if it's not simply because you don't have the help you need. (See Lesson 6.)

*Symptom #2: Doing things that aren't really necessary, regardless of how you do them.* It's one thing to look at a list of things to do today in your independent work and ask whether any of those things can be put off until tomorrow or later. It's quite another to ask if they're really even necessary at all. Ever. Self-employed bookkeeping, for example, is rife with opportunities to create small but time-consuming projects like reports or analysis of little value. (Running another updated QuickBooks® balance sheet, just because you can, is quick as promised; reading it for actionable insights takes longer.)

And then there is email. *Especially* email. (Is it really necessary to respond to that client's or supplier's email response to mine, or is that just what I needed to know and could have thanked them in advance?) One reason email is such a stubborn time sink is that it usually doesn't make it onto any list; it just pops up and demands your attention throughout the day like a circling swarm of gnats that won't go away. Before you know it you're on autopilot, responding to the response and interrupting something more important.

*Symptom #3: Fleeting but extreme self-satisfaction.* Here's a red flag after the task: you're too proud of the way you painstakingly worded that email. (So proud, in fact, that you re-read it after you sent it, and gloated.) Maybe you imagined that the consequences of imperfection were greater than they actually were. In any case, chances are that you spent too long on it—out of proportion to objectives and risks.

Earlier that day you also decided to spend more time on something than you had originally planned to because "it's worth it." Is it? Or is there underlying insecurity telling you that you better over-deliver because under-delivering is too risky. Turns out that recurring over-delivery is at least as risky over time, making your business less profitable and generating stress that reduces capacity and undermines your health. But never mind that, because when you finished that task you strutted like a rooster—so sure that the client will be beyond dazzled. Beyond dazzled can be a wonderful thing, but "beyond" is also a flag. Maybe just dazzled is plenty.

*One more lens.* We could just as well call the Perfectionism Audit the "Is-This-Really-Necessary Audit," whether it's auditing the necessity of the task or auditing the way you're doing it. Don't just take my word for it. One of the most time-honored pillars of executive coaching is a quadrant map called the Time Management Matrix, popularized in the perennial best seller, *The Seven Habits of Highly Effective People.* (Stephen Covey again. Of course, as he pointed out, we're not really managing time—we're managing ourselves.) The matrix divides projects into four buckets: (1) important and urgent; (2) important and non-urgent; (3) urgent but not important; (4) not urgent and not important. There may be justifiable room for more perfectionism in bucket #2, but too much will slow you down in bucket #1 (and in #3, though #3 is not important!). And bucket #4 (which should maybe just go away altogether) is the last place on earth that you can justify perfectionism. So whenever you catch yourself trying to be perfect, make sure you know what bucket you're in. If it's not #1 or #2, you're busted.

*Remember to audit on two levels.* We've now seen that monitoring and managing perfectionism requires vigilance on both the macro and micro levels. At the macro level, is this task even necessary or is it a perfectionism red flag? At the micro level (once the task is deemed necessary), is your effort and attention to detail out of proportion to the task? That brings us full circle back to Covenant 5.

## Calling It Out

*We will diligently monitor the presence of perfectionism that is out of proportion to the task at hand,* **call it out** *when we see it, and adjust behavior accordingly. But if you don't see it, you can't call it out. Monitoring requires ongoing in-the-moment self-awareness.*

This is where mindfulness training comes in. I cover mindfulness and meditation in Lesson 10. But whether you formally practice mindfulness internally or use external "reminder cues," or both, mindfulness is hugely helpful in monitoring your work style and perfectionism in real time. After all, real time is what mindfulness is—being present in the moment instead of the two places where our minds spend most of their time: the future and the past. Is this task necessary *now*? Is the way I'm doing this task *now* aligned with its importance (or lack thereof) and with the real requirements for accuracy, detail, or articulating a point?

If your preference is for external cues, some simple reminder tools can help. The simplest app on my iPhone is an hourly chime (or male or female voice if you prefer, announcing the time). I make sure my sound is turned on when I'm not in a meeting or on a call. Every time that chime rings it's a reminder to check in with myself: how important is what I'm doing right now, and how I'm doing it on the continua of perfectionism and simplicity. There are many variations of this app, and you may want to set one to nudge you even more frequently than hourly in the early stages of your independent adventure.

### Adjusting Behavior: Inserting the "Perfectionist's Micro-Pause"

Congratulations on raising your self-awareness. But what about the final parse of Covenant 5—*behavior modification*. Unfortunately, even in the bliss of mindfulness there can be serious slippage between awareness and action. If you see perfectionism and call it out, nothing changes unless you steer your behavior at a different angle. It's a little like climate change: we can believe in the science, see the devastation caused by storm surges, droughts, and unprecedented wildfires, be of good intention, but still not even turn down the thermostat by a degree (much less put solar panels on the roof). Likewise with perfectionism in independent work: we know we're perfectionists, we know that in many contexts it has diminishing returns, but we're still doing it anyway.

So let's drill down on this. Email is a great place to start, for two reasons. First, you likely do it multiple times every working day depending on the nature of your work. Second, each email written or responded to is a process, and processes are stepwise and tangible enough to be altered. So, Step 1: Is this email or reply really necessary? If so, when you click (Step 2) on that "New Email" or "Reply" button in Microsoft Outlook or Apple Mail, or the "Compose" button in Gmail, turn that into a behavior-check trigger. As soon as you (Step 3) have filled out the "To" (and "cc") fields and the Subject line, Step 4: develop the habit of inserting a micro-pause in the process. It may only be five seconds, no more than ten. Ask yourself whether the combination of this person/these people and the subject are important enough to demand perfection or something close to it. That should be affirmative in only a small percentage of the emails you write or respond to. For the rest, spill what you have to say. Proof it once if it's somewhat important (okay, maybe twice if you need to telegraph the precision of a journalist, copy editor, or language arts tutor, depending on the nature of your work). Send. Then multiply the time you just saved by the number of emails in your Sent box at the end of the day. You'll get a handsome return on those 5-to-10-second investments in micro-pauses.

If all that seems like too much attention on something as pedestrian as email, think of it as a metaphor for any task, no matter how large, in your independent work. Where else can the habit of inserting the perfectionist's micro-pauses be helpful? How about in preparing for meetings? Building the perfect website? What else?

Believe me, I'd be the last person to suggest that you under-prepare for meetings, build a lousy website, or cavalierly send a crucial email with typos and sloppy thinking. I can honestly say that in decades of consulting I believe I've never given a client an incorrect number in an analysis or on an invoice. But I've given them my share of typos even after proofing. It's all about vigilance, tuning into that point of diminishing returns, and trying not to exceed it unless justifiable. (And if it's justifiable, the returns aren't diminishing—gotcha!) That point of diminishing returns is the point of optimization, and optimization of how you spend your time is a pillar of being the best that you can be.

One of the great rewards of well-managed independent work is how efficient you can become, often in sharp contrast to how efficient you were as a company employee. Even Peter Drucker, a giant among corporate management gurus, wryly observed, "Most of what we call management [in companies] consists of making it difficult for people to get their work done." Don't let perfectionism undermine your liberation from company-imposed obstacles to efficiency and productivity.

One last note on this topic: I'm not sure I fully realized the folly of perfectionism until stumbling upon an old book on philosophy in the New York Public Library. While one could argue whether Nietzsche or Plato is the father of perfectionism (they both had plenty to say about it), there has been broad agreement through the ages that perfection does not exist in reality—only in the realm of thought. As Nobel physicist Stephen Hawking, channeling Plato, said, "One of the basic rules of the universe is that nothing is perfect. … Without imperfection, neither you nor I would exist." Yet here we are. In most endeavors, perfection is a mirage. So why spend your hours pursuing something that doesn't exist? Aristotle probably had it right in suggesting we adjust our standards. Know when good enough is good enough, or when "great as it can possibly be" is justified. You'll have more time for making the important things great if you're not trying to make the unimportant things better than they need to be.

Next comes what may be the biggest test of letting go of perfection: getting the help you need to make your own independent working time higher-value time. That brings us to Lesson 6.

\* \* \*

# LESSON 6

◆

## Get the Help You Need Even If You Think You Don't Need It

◆

*"You can do anything, but not everything."*
~ David Allen

*"Although no man is an island, you can make quite an effective raft out of six."*
~ Simon Munnery

Paul Simon once called "I Am a Rock" the most neurotic song he ever wrote. Yet even that self-employed songwriter extolling (with ironic wit) the virtues of isolation, and proclaiming that a rock feels no pain and an island never cries, needed Garfunkel for a time. Some pain (and possibly tears) is an inevitable accompaniment to the joys of working independently. But you need not be a purist on the definition of "independent." A lot of independent workers don't believe they need, or can afford, any help. Until they have it. And that brings us back to Covenant 6: *We will get the help we need before the lack of it materially degrades our performance.*

Independence has its limits. And as with perfectionism, there are symptoms that tell you when you reach those limits. When observing yourself, watch for the two most common of these symptoms (both of which require explanation, even though they are two of the five most basic human afflictions—as well as the basis for many of Shakespeare's plays, countless novels and movies, and bad behavior everywhere in every century): *fear* and *greed*.

## Fear and the Control Freak

If there was a Control Freaks Anonymous 12-step program to be found down the hall from the Perfectionists Anonymous meeting, I should have been in that too. Maybe I still should be. But my freakishness has taught me some things.

When considering getting help for your self-employed self, it usually feels like the opposite of gaining more control. Especially before you actually get that help. The prospect of relinquishing control to a new variable introduces more uncertainty for sure. Yet the ultimate paradox in independent work is that you definitely would not be self-employed if you fear uncertainty! Still, early in my self-employment I feared help as if it were a threat. If only I could have a do-over for those years.

When I left my last salaried executive position to start a new consulting business, overnight I went from having the help of an entire organization and an executive assistant to being utterly alone. Great, I thought. On my own now, I'll finally have everything done exactly the way I want. Then, even as a sole proprietor, I was quickly confronted with more than a dozen additional federal, state, and local tax returns and mandatory compliance forms each year—not to mention having to learn bookkeeping and how to use bookkeeping software. At times it can feel like the administrivia of running your own business is preventing rather than helping you actually deliver a service or product. On those days the drudgery can make you feel less like an entrepreneur and more like entremanure.

Getting the help you need, depending on the nature of your business, may also need to extend well beyond administrative chores. Among my lessons learned were those that came from early consulting engagements in which I had to facilitate full-day strategy workshops in conference rooms with ten to twenty managers seated around the table. I not only had to guide the discussion as facilitators do, managing the flow of conversation and debate, but also was frantically scribing key points and outcomes on easel pads and whiteboards while trying to catch everything that was said and distill it to its essence. These solo outings were incredibly demanding, and very stressful. A friend finally convinced me to sub-contract a "graphics recorder"—someone skilled at, and dedicated solely to, capturing highlights of the discourse in the room. I had resisted because I figured that by the time I explained everything that I needed, and the basics of the client's business, I might as well just do it all myself. Plus, I would have to convince the client to pay for this help or pay for it myself. Eventually, I had to confront the fact that, like a lot of other self-employeds, I had indeed become a control freak. But I also had to admit that facilitating these sessions alone was exhausting. I finally took the plunge and hired Karen, very experienced in facilitation support, for one of my workshops.

When I did, two things happened. The first was noticing how much better her summaries were than mine. They were crisper, more visual, and captured some important details that I'm pretty sure I would have otherwise missed or forgotten. The second thing occurred a couple of days later while reading through Karen's workshop notes and reflecting on the session as I began to write an analysis for the client. I can only describe the feeling as akin to a near-death experience (though obviously less serious) that I had late one night when driving on an unlit portion of the San Diego Freeway in a rural area just south of Orange County, California. There were few cars at that hour and I was comfortably humming along at (or most probably just slightly above) the speed limit. Suddenly I realized that a car with no lights was stopped right in the middle of the freeway, and in my lane. By the time I processed that, I was only within a few car lengths of him and still at 70 mph when I swerved at the last second and went around him on the shoulder. Surprisingly, I remained relatively calm during all that and maintained good control of my car. Then, about a minute later, my knees started shaking uncontrollably. I was a jumble of nerves for a few minutes until I calmed back down.

Though my post-workshop experience was less dramatic than the freeway incident, when I looked back on the workshops I had done completely alone I was horrified that I had taken those on without help. I suddenly didn't see how one person could do all that, and it was now clear that I shouldn't have. And as I pondered whether I would ever do that again, that knee-shaking feeling was just present enough that it actually made me think of the freeway incident (from two decades earlier!) for the first time in many years.

Control-freak fear is not only related to outcomes. It's also related to process. With bringing in help there is fear of it all starting to become more like your old job, when you were supervising people or cajoling your peers to do things your way or what you thought was a better way. Maybe you were even correcting, or compensating for, their mistakes. But like any good investment, the time and energy you put into getting help, and the money you part with initially, will deliver a handsome return if you choose people and tasks carefully.

Some of the most important help you can get may even be free. I can't overemphasize how important it is to have one or more mentors and/or advisors that help you with three critical aids: expertise, objectivity, and feedback. Think about your current and past relationships, personal and professional, and scan them for potential sources of such help. Reaching out is seldom a sign of weakness; quite the contrary—it's showing your smarts and that you're secure enough to show your respect for what you don't know.

And finally, control-freak fear can often also be related to both perceived and real cost. In Lesson 1 I warned that your new boss (you) might be even stingier than your old boss. Let's take a closer look at how this dynamic plays out in failure to delegate when appropriate.

## Greed and the Cheap Boss

I ultimately had to confront another ugly truth: one reason I waited so long to delegate was greed. In the early days of a new business, revenue can be hard to come by. Sharing it is generally not at the top of one's list. And getting help can often seem like an open-ended financial liability. After all, your own overtime doesn't show up on the books (at least not directly), but your help's overtime does. The reasons why that is shortsighted are embedded in that little parenthetic phrase "at least not directly." Nowhere on a balance sheet, among the list of liabilities, will you see a line item for "Burnout Cost" or "Stress-Related Productivity Loss." Nor will you see one for "Inferior Results" (as that will show up silently on the income statement, in lower net profit numbers).

But paying for help doesn't have to be open-ended. If it's for a specific project, arrange a fixed fee. If it's ongoing, set a limit on how many hours you're willing to pay for and stick to it unless it's a clearly justified and rare spike in needs that maintaining or winning an important client/customer relationship depends upon—in which case you'll likely get that extra money back and then some.

## Choosing What to Delegate, and to Whom

There's a Bob Mankoff business cartoon called "How to Delegate During a Recession," in which the company boss says to an underling, "You're fired. Pass it on." At the very beginning of your independent journey, and sometimes even much later, there's no one to pass anything on to. Unless you're firing yourself, you may well need to find slices of the work to delegate.

So, what part of the load to share? That obviously depends on the nature of your business. In any given cycle of work, look at a pie chart of how you're dividing up your own time. For me, as a strategy consultant, that chart for one major project looked similar to the one on the next page.

PROJECT XYZ

- CLIENT RELATIONSHIP MANAGEMENT [10%]
- PROJECT-RELATED READING [5%]
- RESEARCH [10%]
- ANALYSIS [15%]
- CLIENT MEETINGS AND PREPARATION [20%]
- WORKSHOP DESIGN AND FACILITATION [10%]
- DEVELOPMENT OF RECOMMENDATIONS AND PRESENTATIONS [20%]
- ADMINISTRATION (CONTRACTS, TIME AND EXPENSE TRACKING, INVOICING/BOOKKEEPING, TRAVEL BOOKINGS, ETC.) [10%]

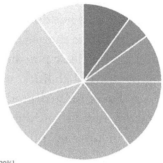

In the example above, I'm embarrassed to say that in earlier years there were similar projects in which I did everything, and I mean everything, myself. In later years, I realized that some of the research, workshop preparation, facilitation support, and administrative work were not high-value uses of my time or experience. Delegating those portions gave me back at least 20% of my time, with a far smaller dilution of revenues and better outcomes for the client.

For each slice of your own pie, estimate the percentages that add up to 100% of total project hours. It's just an estimate and the unknowns may be many, but take your best shot. Then for each slice, dig deep when you ask, *"Is this the best use of my talent, experience, time, and energy?"* On the measure of that question you can score each slice on a scale of 1 to 5, with 1 being the least best use. Then look hard at any 1's or 2's and ask the question again. If the answer is no, you just became your own human resources director: it's time to get help.

### Three Ways to Get Help

Let's talk about the three most basic ways to share your load: hiring, contracting, or partnering with a partner company or individual(s). For the "arms and legs" required just to get stuff done administratively (much of which also requires quite a good brain), it comes down to a choice between hiring someone or using one or more freelancers. (The latter obviously tends to be a better fit to support you in one-time or occasional things like event planning or special meeting facilitation, or very occasional administrative support.)

Hiring is a daunting commitment, especially early on, yet has clear advantages over contracting in many circumstances—even if a part-time hire. But depending on the nature of your business, chances are you can get the help you need from independent contractors. Freelance talent has never been so available as in this blossoming gig economy, and is further facilitated by the growing number of online marketplaces such as upwork.com, freelancers.com, and virtualemployees.com.

So, hiring vs. contracting: which will be best for you? There is much nuance to this debate that's beyond the scope of this book. But a general high-level recap of some basic pros and cons of each is worthwhile here.

Hiring gives you more consistency and dependable continuity in the work being done. You have more control, both in terms of setting hours and deadlines, and a better chance of having things done your way (even if that's not always the best way) rather than training a parade of freelancers. A higher level of trust and loyalty can be developed. And if your business depends on confidentiality, it's easier to secure data and proprietary knowledge with a trustworthy and loyal employee than when sharing it externally. Besides, if you're planning to scale your business rather than be a sole practitioner, hiring staff becomes imperative pretty early on.

On the other hand, for those of you who plan to stay small and like it that way as long as you're meeting your financial objectives, freelancers provide you with obvious flexibility and often better outcomes. You can more easily ramp up and ramp down during busy and less busy periods, respectively. Perhaps most importantly, you can contract the best available person for each task, without the fixed cost of employees or the significant administrative burden that comprises more tax complexity, employee labor laws compliance, potential overtime exposure, and providing benefits. (All of which varies by country, and sometimes even by municipality.) Freelancers will generally have their own office space (even if at home) and pay for most if not all of their own supplies. They can be terminated at any time for any reason, subject to any countervailing provisions in the contracting agreement.

Again, so much depends on the nature of your business as well as your aspirations for it. For many of us in professional services/consulting, we can sometimes find the best of both worlds in a freelancer who is willing to commit a minimum number of hours and is stable enough over a long period of time to be available only when needed. This works particularly well when the help you need is fairly homogeneous in nature and somewhat repetitive, but less well when varied tasks require very different skills.

Then there's the third kind of help, usually in addition to, rather than in place of, hiring or contracting: partnering with another company or individual with complementary skills, clients, or customers that you haven't had access to. Or they may even have useful-to-you intellectual property (inventions/creations ranging from business processes to software to designs, with rights protected by patents or copyrights or trademarks). You may have to get some traction on your own first, but as your business gets more established this is a great way to broaden your opportunities and the footprint of your business without having to build an organization. As a sole practitioner, I have had powerful partnerships with two large global consulting firms, a smaller boutique Silicon Valley consulting firm, a software company, and a virtual global network of consultants and other individual practitioners. I can't overstate how valuable those partnerships have been. I also can't overstate what a minefield they can be if you don't know what to look for and pitfalls to avoid. We will delve into all that in the next chapter.

Before leaving this one, however, I should mention a fourth kind of help: mentors. Yes, we all need more arms and legs to get stuff done sometimes, but from time to time we also need guidance and wisdom from people who have been there and done that (or at least something related). It's lonely at the top, and when you start working independently you're the top even when you're cleaning the toilet. Having a mentor is one of the great antidotes for that loneliness. But loneliness aside, a mentor's guidance and feedback fuels better decisions. Assuming your business is too small for a board of advisors, much less a board of directors, don't let your ego believe that you're just too damned smart to learn from someone else's deep experience or to benefit from their objectivity.

I've had the good fortune to be on both sides of mentoring, as mentor and mentee, and it's a beautiful thing in either direction. I can't tell you how much it helped and how much it meant to me that a seasoned executive coach nine years my senior took me under his wing—not as a client but as a friend who believed in me, cheered me on, and gave me tools to better understand both myself and the people who inhabit my business and personal worlds.

So, you are not a rock. You are not an island. Getting the help you need can even boost your credibility ("She has an assistant; she must be doing pretty well.") It is not an admission of weakness. Under many circumstances, it's just plain smart—and an important part of self-preservation and being at your best. It is not a blight on your self-employed character or reputation or abilities. But burnout is.

\* \* \*

# LESSON 7

◆

# Choose and Manage Relationships Carefully

◆

*"It is better to be alone than in bad company."*
~ George Washington

*"Assumptions are the termites of relationships."*
~ Henry Winkler

In the last chapter we focused mostly on hiring and/or contracting the help you need, with a passing reference to partnering—forming alliances—with other companies or individuals. Partnering is so packed with opportunities and problems that it deserves a deeper dive. So here we are.

But first we should address other non-employee relationships, which may also influence whether partnering is a good idea for you. Whether or not you partner with anyone, you'll be managing external relationships. There are customers/clients, first and foremost, as well as professional services experts (legal and accounting/tax, primarily). Who, and how, you choose can make all the difference between ending up successful and supported or miserably stressed-out and struggling. Sounds like an easy choice between outcomes, right? It's just that *getting the wrong help can be so much worse than getting no help at all.* Want to see my scars and bruises from that? You'll see a few in this chapter, but not without also seeing some thrills and benefits from choosing wisely.

Meanwhile, we start with customers and clients (the appropriate terminology varying with the nature of your work). Because whatever you call 'em, you can't live without 'em.

## Customers/Clients

Back to Peter Drucker, the management mentor to countless CEO's: he famously pronounced that the purpose of any company is to create customers. But fortunately, today an increasing number of companies are recognizing that they also have a higher purpose than customers and profits alone: a responsibility to society to earn their social license to operate by attending to their impact on the environment, the communities in which they work, and the greater good. Still, having no customers or clients equals no business. Whether you will be choosing your customers or they will be choosing you depends on the nature of your independent business. If you're selling something online to a broad audience, they will mostly be choosing you. But if you're in professional services, for example, it's likely that you will be choosing your clients.

Given the greater control in choosing clients than you may have in choosing customers, it's worth exploring control while keeping in mind its relevance to what kinds of customers you may want to target or to avoid in marketing your new business.

I have been blessed with clients over the years who by and large have been very smart, respectful, appreciative, and mostly reasonable. I know this not only in the absolute, but also by contrast—as just like horrible bosses made me appreciate the great ones in the employed phases of my career, the only two unreasonable clients I've ever had among hundreds of individuals underscored how reasonable and appreciative all the others were. (And who's to say what's "unreasonable" if you get paid well enough, though I would nominate the client who said, "You did everything we asked and did it really well, but now we've changed our mind about what we wanted and we're not happy with the work.")

I don't want to skew this book too heavily toward professional services businesses just because I have one. If you're planning on making a business of selling things on eBay or driving for Uber, you may want to skip ahead now to the next chapter. But whether you're contemplating a graphic design business or painting houses, or becoming a life coach or personal trainer, or hanging out a shingle as an independent CPA or investment advisor, you still control whose business you will and won't accept. So stay with me here.

Working independently, you will inevitably have the "soft" quarter (or even year) when any business coming your way—even from jerks—looks very attractive. And when the rent is due, metaphorically or literally, you gotta do what you gotta do. That said, here are eight things to look for in client selection/screening, each explained in more detail below:

- Authority (and the funds!) to hire you
- Integrity (here's where references help)
- Clarity of objectives in working with you
- A business that interests you and that you know something about (though the latter is not always necessary)
- Responsiveness
- Referenceability
- Likeability (including manners)
- Repeaters!

Let's explore each of these.

**Authority and funding.** Nothing is more fundamental, yet this bears repeating even for seasoned service providers. If consumers are your clients/customers, no problem. But if you serve businesses that are companies of any size, it can be shocking how often someone will make overtures about offering you a project—only to have it turn out that, after you've invested time in talking with them, they are not the decision-maker. Either their boss or other colleagues have to sign off, or they have no budget for you yet. Or both. So qualify them early, during that initial meeting or conversation. This can be as simple as saying, "May I ask if hiring me/us is your decision to make?" Accepting their answer on face value leads us directly into the next paragraph.

**Integrity.** Unfortunately, it's too late to find out that a client is lacking integrity by the time they prove it. What legendary investor Warren Buffett said about hiring people applies just as well to clients: "Look for three qualities: integrity, intelligence, and energy, and if they don't have the first the other two will kill you." Yet if you're a small business or solo self-employed, it's highly unlikely that you'll be conducting "integrity interviews" like the ones designed to trick people into telling the truth about their values and past misdeeds. So whenever possible try to speak with others outside the company who have worked with your prospect. (Also a convenient opportunity to ask if they got paid on time!)

**Clarity of objectives.** It's tempting, especially in challenging economic times, to take on a client that knows they need help even if they're not clear on what kind of help they need. It's one thing to help that client clarify their objectives in initial conversations. It's quite another to realize, once you're into the work, that the client's poor communication (or his/her own confusion) has set you up to disappoint them. Sometimes when clients are overwhelmed, they reach out recklessly for help before they have clearly articulated their challenges, prioritized them, and thought carefully about which ones can be effectively addressed with the resources they already have. If you find yourself working too hard to define the problem, that's usually an early warning that you'll be working too hard to solve it. Or you may even end up being a "hammer looking for a nail," doing what you do best when that isn't really what they need. Either way, it's a lose-lose.

**A client that excites or at least interests you.** A luxury, perhaps? Or a chance to do your best work? On one of the occasions that I had to choose between two clients when I was too busy to take on more than one new project, the choice was between a small company that makes recording studio equipment and a much larger one that makes industrial drilling equipment. I know nothing about drilling beyond the dentist, but I'm a musician who loves to record and engineer recordings. For the larger consulting project (and much more money) I would have had to do a ton of reading just to understand what the drilling client's products and those of their competitors really do (and don't do), and how to help them. Upstream all the way. But I already knew my way around the recording process and had worked with several audio equipment manufacturers, and couldn't wait to learn more. Choices aren't always that clear, of course, but it's harder to bill a client for all of your time if you have to spend a lot of it playing catch-up. Plus, it's more fun to look smart in front of clients than to look clueless.

**Responsiveness.** Some very smart, high-integrity clients who know what they want can still be endlessly frustrating for you if they can't respond in a timely manner to things that are needed to keep your project moving. I've certainly had a few—the ones that demand speed and a precision timeline for completing a project, and then don't respond to your emails for a week while you're waiting for more information or approval to proceed to the next step. If you're in a service business, be sure to include a clause in your agreement reminding the client that timely completion is dependent upon timely access to them, timely response, and timely decisions. "Hurry up and wait" may have originated in the military, but it's also very much alive in the business world.

**Referenceability.** If your business is one that would benefit by having clients that other prospects may have heard of, or better yet, even admire, that's at minimum a great tiebreaker when deciding who to target. There are hundreds of small software startups that almost no one has heard of except their customers, but on their websites you will see prominent displays of their well-known customers' logos. I have a cybersecurity software client now with only a few dozen employees that very few big company prospects know about, but their software is already being used by Lockheed Martin. When prospects are directed to the company website and see the

Lockheed Martin logo listed among customers, they instantly know that no one sells cybersecurity software to one of the Pentagon's major defense contractors unless the product is truly excellent. Similarly, when prospects visit my own website and see a long list of market-leading clients, or a formal partnering relationship with one of the world's largest global consulting firms, they're less likely to care that they didn't know about me before—and may even wonder why not. Referenceable customers are worth their weight in gold, which is why it's sometimes good business to be flexible on your pricing in order to win them.

**Likeability.** This one may be a bit age-dependent. *Your* age, not the client's. When I was young and very hungry, I had a much higher tolerance for jerks. Show me an interesting company that I thought I could help and charge a good rate, and if they met any of the other criteria above I could look the other way if they were rather unpleasant, egotistical, and just plain … well, let's just say severely lacking in interpersonal skills. Client likeability never shows up on your income statement, so how important could it be? But over the years, it's become a key driver of life quality for me. I no longer work with clients that I can't enjoy having a meal, a beer, or a glass of wine with. It's human nature to want to help make someone you like be a hero in their business or their life, so liking a client feeds motivation—which in turn feeds success. And in business coaching, the best coaches I've ever known will tell you that they *love* all of their clients. Clients feel that love. It can be very hard to pass up a jerk with a checkbook when you're just starting out. But unless the rent or mortgage is due and you can't make it, resist the temptation. You'll never do your best work for a jerk. And even if you did, a jerk will seldom fully appreciate it. (Or won't tell you even if they do.)

**Repeaters.** An oft-repeated adage in business is that it costs ten times more to acquire a new customer than to keep an existing one. Marketing is expensive. If you take care of your existing customers or clients, you'll save a lot of time, effort, and money in building your business. But that's only half the story. The other half, especially in a service business, is how you can hit the ground running on new projects when you know the client and know how they think, what they value, and their strengths and weaknesses. In addition, you will have already proven yourself, and you'll already know something about their business. So repeat clients/customers, especially if you like them, will almost always be more downstream for you in multiple ways. If a prospective client were to say to me, "If you've been consulting for 30 years, why have you only advised about 50 companies—that's not even two a year?," I would truthfully say that it's because I've been blessed with so much repeat business that I've had more than a half dozen separate engagements with many of those companies. Those relationships are deep and extremely efficient and productive. And don't forget how often people change jobs these days. One of my clients has hired me at six different companies that he's worked for over the years. So priority one, once you get rolling, is taking care of who you've got. And when you're screening new opportunities, think about whether a project looks like an idiosyncratic one-off or an entry point into a customer that could use your services in multiple contexts over time.

A final word on two of these criteria: integrity and likeability. Both have proven to be all-important (in that order) as criteria not just for clients/customers but especially for external partners/collaborators. Even if you could stand collaborating with someone who has great capabilities but questionable integrity and the likeability of a dead skunk, to your clients/customers you're only as trustworthy as your least trustworthy partner. And you're only as likeable as your least likeable partner if they are also customer-facing. On the other hand, while integrity is obviously paramount for your legal counsel and your CPA or accounting service, you may be able to hold your nose on likeability if they're great at what they do—which is far more important. QuickBooks and LegalZoom can be just fine for certain independent businesses (I've used QuickBooks myself for years), but for heaven's sake please don't scrimp on two of the most important investments you'll ever make in your business: sound legal and tax advice.

## Partners, Alliances, and Collaborators

Partners/collaborators—you *can* live without 'em, but you may not want to. At least not entirely. By definition, your new venture will start out very small. And you may want to keep it that way forever if you're successful on your own. I passed up opportunities to build out a global consulting firm with real scale because I so enjoyed the control and flexibility and nimbleness of having just two colleagues—each a sole proprietor. An informal structure allowed us to easily come together to seamlessly serve clients when a combination of our skills and availability was in the client's best interest. Yes, the money would have ultimately been much greater had I built a larger firm, but after managing a division of a large corporation I knew that people management and office politics were not my favorite things. So duplicating those in my own business was off the table.

But there are ways to get some scale, complementary skills or services, and broader access to sales opportunities without hiring. Partnering with larger complementary businesses is one way. Such alliances can take many forms, whether informal or formally contractual. As a sole proprietor, for collaboration I have had contractual relationships with four consulting firms, ranging in size from eight employees to 240,000 (the world's largest professional services firm at the time). These partnerships have been very fruitful, each for different reasons. But, like most relationships of any kind, none were without headaches. So while I consider them all to have been net positive, I feel an obligation to share both some pros and cons.

**Why partner?** A fair question, since you may be leaving or have left a job to get out from under other people's decisions. So why would you invite others into your own bubble of a self-employed adventure? Four reasons, which I like to think of as the "4 S's" of partnering: *scale, synergy, self-educating,* and *sharing*.

*Scale.* What if one of your key reasons for working on your own is to avoid scale and the problems that come with growing a business? Scale can still be beautiful and powerful beyond the revenue, bringing your product or service to a much broader audience and letting you paint your ideas and talent on a larger canvas and with a more colorful palette, without ever building an organization. When you start working independently with little or no brand awareness, leveraging a better-known partner's brand also saves a lot of marketing dollars and effort. Depending on the nature of your business, it can save you the persistent indignity of hearing prospective customers or clients say what a grumpy prospect said in a famous old McGraw-Hill advertisement in business publications:

> *"I don't know who you are.*
> *I don't know your company.*
> *I don't know your company's product.*
> *I don't know what your company stands for.*
> *I don't know your company's customers.*
> *I don't know your company's record.*
> *I don't know your company's reputation.*
> *Now — what was it you wanted to sell me?"*

(If working alone, just substitute "you/your" for "your company" in the above.)

In partnering with larger consulting firms, for example, I suddenly had access to some of the world's largest companies where I had no contacts but my partner firm was a trusted resource. I also suddenly had a global footprint while still operating out of my home office.

*Synergy.* There are situations in which you may have a valuable but incomplete solution to a customer's or client's problem. Partnering with the right complement can complete that solution. Soon after developing a method for companies to use in prioritizing new product development projects, I realized that the process would uncover certain operational challenges that a client would soon encounter but that I was not equipped to advise them on myself. But by partnering with a well-known specialty consulting firm solely focused on product development and operations, we were able as a team to jointly deliver high-value recommendations to clients for not only optimizing their product development investments but also pre-emptively addressing the operational challenges that lay ahead in bringing those products to market. Likewise, some independent tax accountants who are not investment advisors have mutually beneficial relationships with Certified Financial Advisors. Without forming a company together, they can service clients of either business with a complement of tax and investment advisory services. Synergies like these examples can be the big difference between happy clients/customers that stay with you for years and the ones that walk away when you have to say, "Sorry, I can't help with that."

*Self-educating.* Though we're about to discuss some potential headaches and challenges in partnering, one of the great offsets to those is how much you can learn from the right partners. Even with nearly 30 years' experience before I partnered with that largest of professional services companies, five years of that partnership was like getting a couple of additional post-graduate degrees bursting with practical real-world experience. I was suddenly collaborating with an array of senior consultants with deep expertise in a half dozen complementary fields adjacent to my own. We taught each other, and I became a much more well-rounded advisor to my clients even when working alone. But each night I went home with my sole proprietorship—and independence—still intact.

*Sharing.* One of the least explored aspects of working independently is the loneliness factor. When you have a victory with a client/customer, it's great to have someone to share your triumph with—not to mention having had someone to share the workload with. And if, upon finishing a project, you feel it could have had better outcomes, it's great to have someone to share the responsibility and disappointment with, get feedback, and discuss what can be learned from the experience. The beauty of partnering in certain businesses or on select projects is that in the right circumstances you can have it both ways: the ability to experience the joy of being on a successful team without having a boss. Some of my most satisfying moments came just after leaving a client's conference room with colleagues from my partner firm after delivering an enthusiastically-received presentation of our work. It was not unlike heading back to the locker room with teammates after an important victory on the field.

Two main variables, and how they intersect, are in play here. One is the nature of your business, as some are inevitably more solitary than others. The other is personality, since introverts have a much easier time with more solitary business endeavors than do extroverts. This brings us back to *know thyself.* A writer (with introvert leanings) for a major news organization might be very happy becoming a freelance writer, while one with extrovert leanings might terribly miss collaborating with a couple of other journalists on big stories or spending more time in the buzz of a newsroom. I'm essentially an introvert but, when I went out on my own at age 28 after working in Chicago and San Francisco advertising agencies, I was surprised by how much I missed the "electricity" in the hallways of the agency, excitedly exchanging ideas with smart and energetic people, or sticking my head in someone's doorway to ask, "Hey, what do you think about this?" But again, the nature of the business dictates whether loneliness will offset the benefits of having no boss. Even an extroverted executive coach can be a happy sole proprietor because his/her work is so highly interactive, both with a stream of clients one-on-one and in coaching teams of managers.

**Partnering headaches.** Lest I paint a picture of partnering and collaboration as beds of roses, I must address the dark side. And there can be a *very* dark side. (Hence, Covenant 7 regarding choosing partners carefully, a potential pothole large and deep.) Recall the covenant as we now focus on its second half: *We will choose and manage our external business relationships with the utmost attention not only to strategic fit but also to their net impact on both the internal boss and subordinate, personally and professionally, and always in the context of highest ethical standards.* The potential for dark consequences of not choosing wisely principally resides in three areas: control, process, and compensation.

*Control headaches.* When you partner, you have just relinquished some control over integrity, the quality of work that your business delivers, and sometimes even the direction that a project will take if you and your partner are not completely aligned. I've already hinted at what can happen if there's an integrity breach by a partner. The customer won't care whether it's you or your collaborator if they have been wronged. You will likely be personally stained. Regarding quality, the primary reason to partner in the first place is to improve it. But even when you're very discerning about partner selection, there is always the potential for overpromise and under-delivery. Partners can complicate in ways that reduce your ability to quality-control even your own work. If you don't already know the partner and their work well, their references and track record are your best friends before you commit to a relationship even if it's only for a single project.

*Process headaches.* Okay, so now you have your high-integrity collaborator and the great work that they've proven they're capable of doing. What could possibly go wrong? A few things immediately come to mind. First: bureaucracy. If you're partnering with a larger business, you may have to succumb to some of the same policies and procedures that you were trying to escape when you quit your job. Or worse. Collaborating with my largest partner firm, suddenly my client proposals had to endure the scrutiny of a committee. Guidelines for what could and could not be said in a proposal were stifling and at times unreasonable. And the reputation I had with clients for responsiveness was compromised (though clients were usually understanding that this was a trade-off for getting a diverse all-star team of people working on their problem). Second, bureaucracy's evil twin: speed. Everything (not just proposals) took longer—client contracts, internal meetings, developing presentations, revisions, approvals, and (not least!) getting paid. Third: risk aversion. One luxury of operating alone is the unfettered ability to take calculated risks and do really innovative things. Checks and balances can actually be of great benefit and keep you out of trouble, but make sure your partners/collaborators are not so risk-averse as to stifle your creativity to the point of suffocating it.

*Compensation.* I saved the worst for last. Synergies in capabilities may mean 1+1=3 for your clients/customers, but may more likely mean 1+1 = less than what you're used to being paid for your time. Partnering can involve a lot—and I mean *a lot*—of uncompensated time. Clients/customers don't care how much time you may have spent deliberating with your collaborators in meetings and emails and calls back and forth with them, reviewing each other's work, etc., as long as they don't have to pay for it. And if it's a larger business that you're collaborating with, your presence on the team may reduce their profit margin as well—and some if not all of that will come out of your fee. Plus, if your partner is responsible for invoicing your client (and they usually will be if they are a firm rather than an individual like you), the partner gets paid first and you have to wait for your share to work its way through your partner's accounts payable process. So that's often the one-two punch on comp, especially if you're a time-based business—fewer dollars per hour, and waiting longer for it.

## Net Positive

Given the good, the bad, and the ugly, I still stand by what I implied but didn't explicitly say earlier: partnering with the right collaborators can produce amazing results and provide an exhilarating injection of energy and innovation in whatever you do. Is it worth it? Depending on your business and who you are, with well-chosen partners my answer would generally be a resounding yes. Just proceed with caution! And thoughtfully put guardrails on an excess of uncompensated time. Discuss this ahead to raise your partner's consciousness, and you'll still need to remind them along the way. Otherwise even with the best intentions they may not even realize the impact of overcommunicating with you or asking too much—especially when they're drawing salaried paychecks and may never have been on their own. Finally, when in doubt, err in the direction of protecting your reputation and sanity even if that sometimes means saying no to a project that you want but can't do alone.

Whether you're always working alone, or sometimes with partners, you'll still need to evaluate your own performance. So now we move on to that tricky business in Lesson 8.

* * *

# LESSON 8

# Give Yourself Performance Reviews

*"The trouble with most of us is that we would rather be ruined by praise than saved by criticism."*
~ Norman Vincent Peale

*"There is only one way to avoid criticism: do nothing, say nothing, and be nothing."*
~ Elbert Hubbard

When I still had a boss, I walked into a company conference room one day and saw a Mark Anderson cartoon that someone had taped on the whiteboard. It was a drawing of a performance review meeting in which the boss tells his employee, "It's not that you're underperforming, it's that you're over-failing!" Whatever spin one may put on it, if you're dedicated to your independent business and a reasonably good fit for it, your shortcomings will likely be more nuanced. But confronting them on a recurring basis can make all the difference in outcomes and satisfaction. The absence of feedback from bosses and peers, especially when more constructive than in that cartoon, can be a bigger pothole on the No Boss journey than you may think. Filling that void as best you can will be important.

Legendary CEO of General Electric, Jack Welch, argued that every year a business should fire the bottom ten percent of its workforce based on performance. Many companies have heeded his advice, regularly culling those poor souls who sometimes were less capable but other times were just a very bad fit for their role or their organization. However, when you're on your own and bossing yourself around, even if things are not going well it's hard to fire ten percent of yourself.

Or is it? I have fired ten percent of myself multiple times in my years of independent work. The trick is firing the *right* ten percent—that ten percent you need to let go of, or change, at any given time—identifying what it is about you that is sub-optimizing your work, the fruits of your efforts, and the joy of being on your own. What is that ten percent of you that, at the time you're asking, is holding you back from optimizing progress toward attainment of your drivers of satisfaction that you identified, defined, and prioritized in Lesson 3?

For answers, you'll need a very good mirror—with the courage to look into it with all the objectivity you can muster, and with the perceptiveness to see what can sometimes be hard truths. Recall our Lesson 2 discussion of truth and being honest with yourself in your decision to work independently. Now we move that discussion to the context of your performance in that work, and I'll give you some ways to use your mirror.

If you're reading this book—whether coming from a corporate job, a government job, a factory job, a non-profit job, or even a small business with a boss—you've likely been through some kind of performance review (and, if a manager, have conducted those yourself with the employees you supervised). They are traditionally most often done on an annual basis, though there is a strong case for more frequent feedback. A recent Gallup poll showed that annual reviews inspire only 14 percent of employees to improve. Yet it's surprisingly easy when working independently to get a few years down the track before you realize that you haven't really had a disciplined performance review since you started. No one to give you reviews is one of the great perils of the No Boss journey. So as your own boss *and* head of human resources (even if you're the only resource), you'll need to do it yourself. That explains Covenant 8's call for self-review discipline: *We will give ourselves a performance review at reasonable intervals, in which both the internal boss and subordinate can productively check in on how they are doing in the other's eyes and in their own.*

In management practice, generally accepted cornerstones of a useful performance review include: (1) assessment of your effectiveness during the review period, with feedback on your strengths and weaknesses, (2) progress relative to goals, and (3) setting or updating goals for future performance. Let's explore these through an independent lens. (There are many management books that lay out all the aspects of an effective performance review, so I won't try to do that here. Those books can be great references, but are almost always from a larger organization perspective.) Surgeon General's Warning: some of my advice I did not follow. But self-created headwinds and stepping in potholes have been great teachers, and that's how I know it's good advice (and can spare you breaking an ankle).

## Effectiveness, Feedback, and Meeting (or Exceeding!) Your Goals[2]

Dictionary definitions of *effectiveness*—like "producing a desired result," as found in the Oxford Dictionary—are far too simplistic for performance review purposes. I prefer to think of effectiveness as the combination of *doing the right things* and *doing things right.* In a business organization, broadly speaking, executives tend to be more responsible for identifying the right things to do, while managers tend to be more responsible for getting those things done right. You can think of the former as strategies, and the latter as execution of those strategies.

In a No Boss environment, we're on the hook for both—interdependent conjoined twins, but with different skills. So it's crucial to be very clear-eyed about which is which in reviewing yourself. There were times when I wanted to fire myself (all 100 percent of me) after doing a world-class job on something that I shouldn't have been doing at all, and other times when I saddled myself with a

---

[2] Some of what I've learned about effectiveness is from my own mistakes, but much was also learned from the many mistakes I avoided by having been coached by extremely talented and wise coaches. Special thanks to Lee Franklin of the California Leadership Center for informing this chapter and others.

"great idea" that would be impossible to execute well without more special expertise or an unrealistic amount of time and money. If you're already on your No Boss journey, ask these questions separately: *how have you been doing on identifying the right things*, and *how well have you done them*. We'll get more specific about all that momentarily in discussing five "check-in factors" when reviewing yourself. But first, a bit more about getting to the truth when looking in your performance review mirror.

When coaching clients who are unhappy in work and thinking of either changing jobs or working independently, I've learned the importance of helping them clarify which of their complaints are about things beyond their control. The rest of their problems are often of their own making. Managers who don't "fix themselves" will take those problems wherever they go. I call that phenomenon SDS—Serial Dissatisfaction Syndrome—in which history keeps repeating. Some causes of SDS that didn't show up when you had a boss can emerge in independent work, even if one of your great hopes for working independently may be to make them disappear. And they can. But only by using your honest mirror often enough, and having the courage to change.

When I was responsible for too many people as an executive, I simply didn't like how much time I had to spend on people management. Independent work certainly fixed that. But recall in Lesson 1 when I talked about the leather-bound book of lovely handwritten letters that my employees gave me when I left the company, and how that made me realize that I hadn't set effective personal boundaries as a manager. I had found myself listening to personal problems of managers two or three levels below me. I unwittingly took that issue with me into independent work, even with no employees, as in the early years of my business I failed to set adequate boundaries with some of my clients. Then I wondered why I had been feeling that too much of my client time was uncompensated, because I was indulging them in too many "off the meter" conversations or too much preliminary document review before having a signed proposal. I ultimately had to fire that ten percent of myself. But first I had to realize what

I was doing and how that was impacting my work satisfaction and productivity.

There are some things about effectiveness and feedback that are well worth adapting from traditional performance reviews when looking in your independent work's mirror. One is something you likely did to prepare for reviews when you had a boss: make some notes about what you want to discuss. What do you think you've been great at this year? Not so great? (Or even terrible?) What are the big things that bother you, little things that annoy you enough to matter, and opportunities that you would like to take advantage of but haven't? How are you doing relative to your goals and expectations a year ago, and what are your goals and expectations for this next year? (We'll get to goals shortly.)

On effectiveness, strengths, and weaknesses, I found that one way to magnify my mirror for closer self-inspection has been through *journaling*. I know, I know—how will you possibly have time for that? But our psyches are wiser than we know, and if you allow yours to express itself on the written page with its private and honest and unfiltered thoughts about how you're fulfilling your drivers of satisfaction—or not—it can be your mirror. And if you ignore what your psyche is trying to tell you, it will ultimately be relentless in handicapping you until you pay attention.

What, more specifically, would you be journaling about (or at the very least, thinking about) when focusing on effectiveness? There are five check-in factors that I believe, collectively, constitute a healthy look at independent work effectiveness:

- To what degree you're fulfilling your drivers of satisfaction
- How your business results compare to your business goals
- How efficiently you've been operating
- How you've been approaching risk-taking
- Your state of mind during the period being reviewed, and now

*Fulfilling your drivers of satisfaction.* By now you know my conviction about how drivers of satisfaction can and should be guiding lights that illuminate how successful and satisfying your No Boss adventure actually is—and what you should focus on to continually make it better. Return to those drivers frequently, but especially during performance introspection. At the high level, for each driver, even a simple 5-point or 10-point rating scale on which you thoughtfully rate "how am I really doing on this particular driver, relative to hopes and expectations?" can provide a powerful lens on performance in the all-important contexts of meaning and satisfaction. This transforms your subjective judgment and feelings into quantitative outputs. Those outputs can paint a picture of how you may need to shift your focus to pay more attention to some drivers and less to others during the next period. And possibly beyond.

Your drivers of satisfaction are also instrumental in determining whether you're doing the right things, irrespective of whether you're doing them right. Every project or strategy can be evaluated on each of your drivers on the same simple scale as used above. Totaling up the ratings across all your drivers, weighted by the relative importance of each driver as we described in Lesson 3, will tell a story about that project or strategy. For example, I found that taking on a client who couldn't afford my normal consulting rate, but who wanted help in reducing their company's environmental footprint and climate impact, scored poorly on my 'financial security' driver of satisfaction—but scored so well on 'aligns with my values,' 'intellectually interesting work,' and 'working alongside smart, stimulating people' that overall it outscored much more profitable projects that year. Back to doing the right things—right for you—not just doing things right.

*Results compared to goals.* What goals did you set at the beginning of your No Boss adventure (or, if you've been at this a while, at the time of your last self-administered performance review if you did one)? Some goals may be quantitative, like increasing your revenue or number of customers by X percent. Others may be more qualitative, like attracting clients/customers that are more referenceable as discussed in Lesson 7. Since your drivers of satisfaction will likely tend toward subjective criteria, addressing how well you're fulfilling those drivers will have already covered much of the qualitative aspects. So anything quantitative is particularly helpful here, as there is some truth in the old business adage, "You can't manage what you can't measure." (You *can*, however, manage to improve on some things you can't measure, and I've already mentioned several of them).

In any case, just be sure you're doing at least two important things that any well-run business does when tracking performance against goals or targets. First, if you're underperforming, identify why. But also revisit whether that goal, in hindsight, was unrealistic. Then course correct, addressing the "why" with behavior modification. Or, if the goal was overly ambitious, adjust it for the next period. If you're exceeding certain goals, congratulations—but honestly probe whether those goals were ambitious enough or if the bar was set too low. Ideally, all your business goals will be aggressive enough to motivate you to be your best and put you on a satisfying financial trajectory, but not so aggressive as to inflict unhealthy stress, damage self-esteem, or provoke violations of integrity for "success at all costs."

*Operating efficiency.* You may meet someone at a bar or party who boasts about their independent business, "I had a great year—I billed 20 percent more than last year"—without mentioning that expenses were 50 percent higher and that they put in 30 percent more time than in the previous year. In small businesses, there's a tendency to be much more focused on revenue and cash flow than on eliminating unproductive time and expense. In Lesson 5 we discussed how perfectionism can compromise efficiency and time management. In Lesson 6 we discussed delegation—getting the external help you need—so that more of your own time can be higher-value time. So a performance review is a good time to check in on how both of those things are going for you. And if your business is a solo adventure, the business's expenses are all *your* expenses, so that's another quantitative part of your efficiency mirror.

For example, when I first realized that I was getting enough business from word-of-mouth and former clients, and only needed my website to be something I could personally direct those people to for information and reference, I stopped paying for search engine optimization for the site. I didn't need to drive traffic there; I just needed it to be there for already-interested parties. And even before Covid, I substituted more virtual meetings for air travel—reducing expenses by thousands of dollars (and simultaneously reducing my carbon footprint). Don't be fooled by a stock market that every day tells us revenue is sometimes more important than profitability for some companies. Unprofitable revenue is like a fleeting sugar high that can very briefly feed your ego before it makes you feel lousy afterwards for a longer time. When you're on your own and unless you're wealthy, it's only net profit that pays the mortgage or the rent, puts food on the table, and helps set you up for your retirement years.

*Prudent risk-taking.* When Eleanor Roosevelt said, "Do one thing every day that scares you," I'm not sure she had independent work in mind. But it's not bad advice if you'll be bossing yourself around, as you'll have plenty of opportunities to do something scary after that big scary thing called leaving your job. If you're already working independently, you've certainly demonstrated a willingness to take risks. Congratulations! I know many highly capable people who simply don't have the stomach for relinquishing their paychecks, employer health insurance, expense accounts (if they have them), and paid vacation time. Working independently can sometimes feel like walking a tightrope without a safety net, with frequent opportunities to fall to an unforgiving ground. However, there's a fine line between risk, which has negative connotations, and getting outside your comfort zone. The latter can be exhilarating and immensely rewarding psychologically, emotionally, and financially.

Getting outside your comfort zone is supposed to be (duh!) uncomfortable. Think back to the times when you did it. Start way back, thinking about the arc of your life and when you took chances. List at least three to five episodes. In case some examples help, here are three from my own list that range from age 13 to just four years ago. At 13 I tried out for high school basketball as the shortest boy in the whole school. I actually made the team, but knew I would likely be the butt of some jokes. The first time the coach put me in a game, the referee wouldn't let me play because he couldn't read the number 28 on my jersey—since even the smallest jersey was so big on me that the number wrapped around my sides. By the next game I had switched to number 5, the only single-digit jersey available, which merely covered my entire chest but was readable. For further embarrassment, the high school yearbook sports section had a photo of me from the waist up with hands in the air fighting for a rebound with another player; you couldn't see that I was standing on a crate for the photo shoot. Then at age 25, in an interview with the president of a San Francisco ad agency, he asked me where I saw myself in five years and I told him I saw myself at *his* desk in *his* job—not fully aware of how ridiculous that may have sounded, but very nervous saying it nonetheless. Just four years ago, I did a solo two-hour singer/songwriter show at a Seattle coffee house after not performing in public for four decades (and back then was in bands, never solo).

So think back, having heard these examples, with pencil in hand. Maybe you were a shy kid but had to go door to door in sixth grade to sell raffle tickets to raise money for your school. Maybe at 17 you got up the courage to ask the most popular girl—or boy—in the school for a date. Maybe at 29 you agreed to speak at a major conference for the first time, or maybe you spoke up in a meeting of senior executives two levels above you. Or maybe you traveled to a beautiful country where recent civil unrest made things less safe than usual. Whatever episodes come to mind, from being a small child all the way to yesterday, how did they work out for you? Make notes about your triumphs and rewards, your failures and consequences. How did they all net out? Was it worth it?

Yes, I made the basketball team, but people in the visitor stands snickered at me in amusement when I walked onto the court in my baggy uniform and a head shorter than everyone else. (They couldn't know I would eventually be 5'11". Neither could I!) Yes, I got the job at the agency, and was promoted the following year. But before I could find out how short of experience I would still have been in five years to be its chief executive (which I can certainly see now), I left to start an independent work adventure. And yes, I made it through my first solo coffee house show, though I botched some guitar chords and momentarily forgot a couple of lyric lines in the course of doing 26 songs. But people seemed to enjoy it, and I had a blast even while being nervous. Were these risks worth it? Absolutely! Every time it was a significant step forward in personal growth, character building, self-knowledge, confronting some limitations but breaking through others. Each episode felt like a personal victory. I believe you will find the same.

Now, in your performance review, think back through the period that you're reviewing and ask when you stepped out of your comfort zone during that time. If you come up empty handed, your No Boss ship is still safe in the harbor. But as Einstein pointed out, being safe in the harbor is not what a ship was built for. You'll likely be happier and ultimately rewarded if you sail that ship, so keep that in mind when you're setting goals. Just don't get so crazy with risk that you blow up your business (or your personal life) during a major small craft advisory.

*State of mind.* I'll say much more about state of mind in Part III of this book. But for now, let's focus on those moments when you're checking in with yourself. The two things that seemed to most impact my effectiveness over the years, positively or negatively, have been poles apart: *how stressed* I've been and *how optimistic* I've been. My best years have been when I've taken good care of myself, setting boundaries around prolonged overwork, exercising, eating well, meditating, and *trusting* that everything will be all right even if a major project just fell through and I would be without work for weeks or even a couple of months (because in my business it takes time to sell a replacement project). My worst years have been when I either pushed myself too far, or temporarily believed that having a couple of soft business quarters meant that I was losing my touch. So think again about this past year or review period. On a scale of 1 to 10, how stressed have you been? (1 is feet up on the desk sipping your beverage of choice; 10 is hair on fire in a small, dark, windowless room.) How often have you been stressed beyond a 5? How stressed are you right now? There are no right answers; there is only self-awareness, and the hope that you're not running hot enough for your hair to ignite. How optimistic have you been feeling? We'll explore all of this further in Lesson 10: Making It Work for the Long Haul.

## Goal Attainment and Goal Setting

We covered the issue of how you're doing vs. your business goals, but what about personal goals? When I had bosses, like so many bosses they usually wouldn't care much about goals I had for myself outside of the office. Those would be beyond the scope of a performance review, even if some of them would inform my work in some way. And they almost always do. But with self-employment, the lines will inevitably be more blurred between your business and personal life, and even between business and personal goals. Trade-offs can be starker. When I had a boss and an executive assistant and a staff, I knew that things would continue to get done while I was on vacation. But for the last few decades, if I wanted to go sea kayaking on a gorgeous Tuesday (you may have heard that it rains a lot in Seattle, so sometimes we have to take the sun when we can get it), my business paused. I made no money that day, and I knew I was setting myself up for a possibly brutal 14 hours at my desk tomorrow. If I wanted to learn another language, or become a better musician (and keep a guitar within reach of my desk), there would be less time for reading business and technology publications to stay really on top of developments in my clients' industries. Trade-offs abound.

Personal goals are especially subject to getting marginalized when you're tackling the challenges of forging an independent business. One year I took on two large and lengthy projects with difficult clients (remember Lesson 7 on the perils of not choosing carefully?). The weeks turned into months as I was head-down with keeping these projects on track in between frequent bouts of wrestling with clients who were creating problems for me with one hand and paying me top dollar with the other. I had a 'very good' year relative to financial goals and my financial security driver of satisfaction. But when I did my year-end performance review, I was sobered to realize that I had only been in my kayak once all year. Nor had I played much guitar, much less written any new songs. Even with all the ink that has been spilled by people writing books and articles on work-life balance, I can't overemphasize enough the importance of keeping personal goals intact while shouldering the responsibilities of independent work.

Even though your old boss may not have cared much about your personal pursuits outside of business, go forth with the knowledge that those pursuits—with some boundaries around the amount of time you can put into them—will more often than not make your business better. Some of the very best ideas for my clients have come to me alone on the open sea. And songwriting, with its discipline of having only 150 words in which to develop characters and a plot, taught me much about how to concisely present information to busy senior executives in my consulting business. So make sure your No Boss business doesn't become the bottomless pit that it so easily can, as there will always be more to do. Whether you're on a hiking trail, taking cooking classes, investing time in your friendships, learning Italian, or competing on the tennis court, whatever you're doing that "isn't work"—in moderation—will likely be good for your business. Nurturing yourself informs work in mysterious ways, and is great insurance against burnout.

This does *not* mean setting less ambitious goals for your independent business. If you set the bar too low, you won't get to the truth on doing the right things or doing them right. The only times I ever lapsed into sloppy prioritization or inefficiency and still met my business goals were a couple of periods in which, in retrospect,

I probably asked too little of myself. Those years were not only less financially rewarding, but also a reminder of one big difference in performance reviews compared to when you had a boss: before you ask for a raise now, be sure you can afford it!

## Be Disciplined, But Be Merciful

Finally, when reviewing your performance, it's a fine line between self-criticism and self-compassion. It will be tempting to use yourself as a punching bag if things aren't going as well as you hoped. But what you're doing is hard. If it weren't, everyone with a bad boss would be doing it. And that's a whole lot of people who are still employed. So crack the whip when warranted and really do strive for continuous improvement, but applaud yourself for the things you're doing well—and for the fact that you're doing this at all. *No Boss is a hero's journey.* You'll need self-compassion every day, not just during reviews. Every hero has shortcomings and makes mistakes. You're still a hero for breaking out to pursue a dream.

\* \* \*

## LESSON 9

◆

# Know When to End a Marriage (to an Idea)

◆

*"Never give up on something that you can't go a day without thinking about."*
~ Winston Churchill

*"Never love something so much that you can't let go of it."*
~ Ginni Rometty

Who is right—Churchill or Rometty (former CEO of IBM)? This chapter is especially for those who have an idea or vision for doing something truly innovative in their independent work or business, or in the arts with commercial aspirations. Few things are as exhilarating as creating something valuable from nothing. It's a truly seductive experience, both intellectually and emotionally. Ah, but there's the rub: seduction. As award-winning cinematographer and film director Louie Schwartzberg hypothesized, seduction is one of nature's tools for survival because *we will protect what we fall in love with*. That includes ideas.

I only wish I had realized the import of that before marrying myself to two things (besides my wife, which worked out unusually well). One was my patented business process, referenced earlier, that I grandiosely thought would ripple through the global corporate world and change how most companies make decisions about product design and development. The other was songs I wrote that I was convinced should be on the radio. I was seduced by my creations, and spent much of my independent career protecting them. I don't just mean legally protecting them with a patent and more than a hundred copyrights, but protection by sticking with goals related to those ideas past the point of diminishing returns.

No regrets, as these were good marriages for many years. I can't know your ideas or visions, but I hope you will find value in my sharing a few of my mistakes in staying in one of those marriages (in my case, to intellectual property) for too long. So here goes.

## Doubling Down

In recent years the phrase "doubling down" has wormed its way into the English vernacular in many contexts. Whether it's a recalcitrant Senate leader doubling down on blocking the other party's legislative agenda, or a CEO doubling down on investing in an expensive and unproven new technology, it's easy to forget that the phrase originated as a gambling term—in blackjack. High risk, high reward (or catastrophic loss?). In the stock market, investors are tempted daily to double down on shares that have fallen significantly in price since buying them. They look like a real bargain now. Sometimes that can end well, when a good company recovers and ultimately yields a handsome return for its shareholders. Other times it ends very badly, where doubling down by buying more shares more cheaply on their way down turns out to be a futile attempt to 'catch a falling knife' that cuts you badly en route to the floor, where it stays.

It's hard to ever let go of what you believe in your bones is a great idea. And it can be just as hard to know when. When have you fully given it the effort it's due? Or when have you met enough resistance to read the writing on the wall and move on to a different idea or vision? Confronting these questions takes courage, and that is the courage called for in Covenant 9: *We will have the courage down the line and at intervals thereafter to ask and answer whether our original business idea for working independently is still the best idea for our well-being—or whether we need a different (or substantially modified) dream.*

Whether you're just starting an independent business with a great idea, or have just hatched a great idea in an already-established business, I hope you'll never have to decide to let it go. But depending on which of those two situations describes you, whether and when to let go, if ever, is a very different decision. Why? Because some businesses are entirely dependent on the success of a great idea, or even the protection of an invention, while others have a revenue stream that the new idea would be additive to—but the business can still survive or even thrive without it.

## Risks of a Bad Marriage

One big clarification: your idea or vision can indeed be great and even very valuable, but can still turn out to be a bad marriage for you. So as I talk about risks, they in no way imply that your idea is anything less than world-changing and totally unique. But there are three ways that even the best idea in the world can sink your No Boss ship. The first is obvious: draining your capital, time, and energy with, ultimately, little or no payoff due to circumstances beyond your control. The second is less obvious: prospects' inability to grasp the true value of your idea, even if it's clear to you. The third is also less obvious: your idea becomes a "hammer looking for a nail" because every problem starts looking to you like something your idea can solve. Objectivity can be hard in proportion to how great you think your idea is.

Let's explore all three risks, and how your marriage to an idea can impact your independent success or failure.

## Risk #1: Money Pit, Time Pit, Energy Pit

A dire sub-heading for sure, but remember we're talking about risks—and the rewards for assuming those risks can be tremendous. Let's just go in with our eyes open.

First of all, if you truly have a uniquely powerful idea for, or in, your independent business, you'll want to protect it—your intellectual property ("IP")—from being stolen or copied. (Imitation is not only the sincerest form of flattery; it can also be an insincere form of outright property theft.) Sometimes protection will be simple and very affordable; for example, a particular graphic design can be copyrighted for (at this writing) $65 US and various similar fees in other countries. But if your idea is truly an invention, a patent will be the more appropriate way to protect it from emulation or use beyond your control. Patents can be *very* expensive—in both money and time. More on that in a moment.

So, how to know if your idea is just an idea or an invention? I am *not* an intellectual property attorney, so *always* consult with one if there is any doubt. (Like it says on the T-shirt you'll find in law school book stores, "If at first you don't succeed, try doing what your lawyer told you to do the first time.")

An invention is something new and useful that did not exist before. It may be a product, a method, a formula, an algorithm, or any number of novel and useful things that you bring into existence. If you can make a persuasive case for its novelty (or what IP attorneys call "non-obviousness") in the face of all the inventions that already exist, your invention may be patentable. The idea of starting a business with a food truck that serves Jamaican food, even if it's the only Jamaican food truck in town, is an idea—not an invention, even if a really good idea. Creating a unique decision model with never-before-used formulas that were designed to help a company decide what products to make is an invention. (I know this from having been granted a patent on it.) If you create new software or a mobile app, you can copyright the code if you own it and may also be able to copyright certain photos or images that are used within. But if you want protection from someone else creating software, or an app that does the same thing with different code, you may want to seek a patent.

Whatever level of creation you have birthed for your independent business, protect your intellectual property if it's protectable.

But at some point, if you think it's patentable, you will have to decide whether you're willing to sign up for spending what could very easily be six figures in legal fees and patent office fees to get through the gauntlet of complex applications, responding to patent examiners' "office actions" that challenge your case, appealing examiners' rejections, and—if you're lucky enough to be granted a patent—paying significant maintenance fees going forward at certain intervals as required by the patent office. And what I described is just for a United States patent. Worldwide protection is yet another set of gauntlets. And fees. Yet, as big a fan as I am of do-it-yourself on many things, I reiterate that IP protection is something you will usually want to do with experienced legal counsel.

Was it all worth it for me? Yes, even after having to abandon three other patent applications that didn't make it all the way through the gauntlet. I ultimately got more than my money back, though there was certainly no guarantee. And along the way, I at least knew that my invention had some modicum of protection since patent protection is granted retroactively to the date of the first "provisional" application. But I did spend more of my savings on the front end than I ever anticipated, and hundreds upon hundreds of hours not only on my applications and office actions but on reviewing others' related patents to determine the extent of uniqueness of my invention. After all that, and dozens of copyrights, there was no one to ask for compensation for any of that time—only me, bossing myself around.

The overwhelming majority of No Boss adventures may never be dependent on intellectual property protection. So this is for those of you bent on innovating, creating, inventing—or even surprising yourself by doing so. It's a magical way of differentiating yourself in the increasingly crowded field of independent businesses, and differentiation breeds success.

### Risk #2: No One Thinks Your Baby is Beautiful

So you have what you think is a novel idea for stepping out on your own, and you even believe it can make the world a better place—at least for your customers or clients. You work assiduously to develop it, polish it, test it, and maybe even copyright it or apply to patent it if that's appropriate and feasible. Then you take it out into the wider world, ready to dazzle with your genius and your beautiful baby.

You're mystified when the first prospects (or investors) that you show it to don't say "Wow—congratulations—this is amazing!—where do I sign?" Can't they see? But if it's a good idea, targeted to the right people, chances are they don't actually think your baby is ugly. They just don't love it enough to do anything about it other than be polite and tell you that it's really good. Just not for them. Rejection comes with the territory. I'm an expert (from the school of hard knocks) on rejection. I showed my Strategic Harmony® IP to nearly two dozen companies before Hewlett-Packard and Symantec (now Broadcom) became the first clients for it. Some of those rejectors weren't polite. ("We have everything under control and don't need someone to come in here and try to fix something that isn't broken.") My songs were rejected literally hundreds of times in L.A., New York, and Nashville before Harry Belafonte recorded one of them. But I had to remind myself that The Beatles were rejected by more than 30 record companies before they finally got a deal and released "Love Me Do" in 1962. And in business, Alexander Graham Bell's patented telephone in 1876 was met with abject ridicule. (When he pitched it to the president of Western Union, the response was, "The idea is idiotic … why would any person want to use this ungainly and impractical device when he can send a messenger to the telegraph office and have a clear written message sent to any large city in the United States?") So please don't take this discussion of risks as encouragement to abandon your creation. Besides, rejection builds persistence muscles, which you'll need anyway to sustain any business. Use rejection experiences to learn, refine, and improve not just your ideas but also how to talk about them.

To that last point, just as brilliant artists are often not so brilliant at promoting their own work, you may not be the most persuasive spokesperson for your idea or invention. If you don't have that P.T. Barnum marketing gene in your DNA, consider my suggestion in Lesson 6 ("Get the Help You Need Even If You Think You Don't Need It"): how about contracting an articulate business development person who loves sales and lives for the hunt? If you find a talented one who's willing to work on commission or a finder's fee, you can avoid out-of-pocket costs and use your time to further refine your ideas, or create others. I was sure my baby was beautiful, but I was late in discovering that sales was not the highest-value use of my time or talents. (I'm being charitable to myself; there are much better salespeople.) I would do it differently in a do-over.

## Risk #3: A Hammer Looking for a Nail

When it comes to ideas and inventions, objectivity is the hardest thing. Of course your baby is beautiful—it's *your* baby. And it's especially beautiful if it's the singular idea that you're "betting the farm" on for your independent business. But as the French philosopher Chartier said, "Nothing is more dangerous than an idea when it's the only one you have."

Shortly after I started pitching my Strategic Harmony® IP to companies, I realized that in every meeting, I tended to talk too much and listen too little. I wanted them to see, understand, and admire my creation. But it was complex, and could easily take the better part of a one-hour meeting to present. There was too little time remaining to listen to their problems. (Always listen first regardless of what you're presenting.) I'm embarrassed to admit now, all these years later, that I would leave some of those early meetings too clueless about this: why should this company even care about my invention if they believed it would solve a problem that they didn't think they had?

After serial rejections I had to confront that Strategic Harmony® had become the proverbial hammer looking for a nail: every business problem started to look to me like something that my invention could solve. It took restraint and discipline to finally start listening more before I talked. Then I could present a more streamlined, simplified description of my solution in the context of the client's business problems—and know that if I piqued their interest enough there would be a follow-up meeting in which I could go into more detail and even close the sale. After pivoting in that way, it wasn't long before a dozen well-known companies had become clients and implemented my method.

I should have learned this lesson well before my invention when I first began pitching my songs to record producers and record companies—often thinking that whatever I had just finished writing was a potential hit. But if my "casting" (the artist whose producer or record company I was pitching the song to) was off target—insensitive to what they were currently working on and what projects were most in need of new songs—it wouldn't matter how good the song was. So, back to objectivity: in retrospect, the majority of those songs of mine—even the really good ones—were not commercial enough to be "hits" (a rare commodity, though like many songwriters I stubbornly consider some of my unrecorded songs "orphans" that are still waiting for adoption). Bias dies hard.

## Time to Say Goodbye?

Judging when it's time to move on from an idea is much harder if your goals and expectations are fundamentally flawed—either poorly considered and articulated, or miscalibrated to the point of setting the bar far too high. Or too low. If my expectation for the Strategic Harmony® process was to revolutionize the corporate world, I would certainly have to consider it a failure thus far. But as the process's sole salesman and chief implementer, if my goal had been, say, to somehow get ten market-leading companies to implement the process in less than ten years and have them see demonstrably better business results, I could consider it a resounding success when I blew past that goal in Year 7. Likewise, for many years after leaving Los Angeles and songwriting to return to the business world, I considered my seven years there to be a great underachievement because my songs were recorded by only a handful of known artists—in contrast to my initial (and, in retrospect, naïve) expectation of establishing and sustaining a parade of hit songs. Yet ten years after my minor successes, some of the songwriters who had arrived in L.A. with big dreams around the same time as me were still waiting for their first major record and still trying to cobble together a subsistence living. So, did I fail? In that latter context, definitely not. But at the time, disappointment relative to expectations, combined with family considerations, strongly suggested it was time to say goodbye to L.A. and return to a somewhat more predictable business world. You can see how important the context of goals and expectations (as discussed in Lesson 8) are in knowing whether and when to leave or stay in a marriage to a vision, idea, or invention.

On the sunny side, let's assume that your goals are healthy and in focus, and that you're about to marry—or are already married to—an idea. To summarize what I've said about risks: (1) be aware of the risk/reward trade-offs inherent in protecting an idea or invention; (2) be vigilant about loss of objectivity regarding the beauty of your baby (and know that a business development partner who has to sell it can be helpful in that regard too); and (3) listen to your audience before you presume that they're just another nail for your hammer. All of this will help you recognize when a marriage to an idea has become a bad marriage for you, or a marriage that you're staying in too long without the results you're hoping for.

Generally, I don't recommend divorce (I've been married to the same amazing woman for more than 40 years). I certainly don't recommend ever giving up prematurely on a great idea. I'm all for Einstein-like persistence. (He said, "It's not that I'm so smart, it's just that I stay with problems longer.") Its value in weathering the volatility of independent work can't be overstated. So may your great idea exceed your wildest expectations of success. Intend that it will. But if it doesn't, fear not—it won't be your last idea!

* * *

# PART III

## Sustaining Independent Success

## LESSON 10

◆

# Sustaining Independent Success: Making It Work for the Long Haul

◆

*"Self-care is not self-indulgence, it is self-preservation."*
~ Audre Lord

*"If you get tired, learn to rest, not to quit."*
~ Banksy

Your own business at last! It's all on you now. Determined to get that cash flow moving as soon as possible, and keep it that way, it's full speed ahead. Trouble is, full speed ahead with little letup can lead to No Boss burnout more quickly than you might imagine. Of course, as with starting any worthwhile business, there are likely to be heavier burdens and stresses in the beginning. But there are some of us who, unwittingly, tend to keep pedal to the metal relentlessly and long after it's required, healthy, or good for the business. Your new boss (hey, you!) can be even more likely than your old boss to try to suck as much work out of you as the clock and human body will allow. Burnout can easily follow faster than where you used to work.

This is where Covenants 10, 11, and 12 all team up to save you. And sustain you. Re-read them now in the No Boss Contract (Lesson 1). From their collective riches, I offer four strategies to avoid the No Boss burnout trap. I came to all of them late, not truly operationalizing them until the most recent dozen years or so in my independent work. But what a difference they've made!

Simply put, they are: (1) resting (yes, really!), (2) mindfulness, (3) consciousness, and (4) gratitude. I elaborate on each below, in the context of a No Boss existence.

### Rest (Really?)

In 1930, economist John Maynard Keynes wrote a seminal essay predicting that 100 years from then we would be working only 15 hours a week, thanks to technology-enabled increases in productivity. Coincidently, that's about the same number of hours as the hunter-gatherers of the Stone Age, according to anthropologists. But it sure looks like we're not going to make it by 2030. It seems that the more productive we get, the more that's expected of us. In an era of employers making employees do more with less, and squeezing every ounce of inefficiency out of their businesses at the altar of shareholder value, you may already have been conditioned to work harder every year. And now you're giving yourself the ultimate shove—No Boss—with no limits on work ethic other than the ones you impose on yourself. Let's return to the ancient Greeks for wisdom (most of whom, incidentally, were self-employed).

Recall that Lesson 4 began with the Greek inscription for "Know thyself" found on the Temple of Apollo at Delphi. But that wasn't the only inscription there. Below that was ΜΗΔΕΝ ΑΓΑΝ. *Nothing to excess.* That includes work! Prolonged mental activity causes physical exhaustion. I'm not asserting that limiting yourself to no more than 35-40 hours a week, especially in the beginning of launching a new business, is realistic or even the optimum formula for success. I'm simply suggesting (as I reflect on my scars from more 60-to-70-hour weeks than I care to remember) that if you routinely overdo it without sufficient rest, you will pay. Maybe even the ultimate price if you do it for an extended period of time.

And so, what about the long haul? As the phenomenal British marathon runner Ryan Holmes, the youngest person in history to run 100 marathons in a single year, likes to say, "You can run a sprint or you can run a marathon, but you can't sprint a marathon."

And unless you plan to go back to letting someone else boss you around, independent work is definitely a marathon.

Before young Mr. Holmes had learned to walk, much less run, I tried to sprint a marathon for years until I hit a wall akin to post-traumatic stress syndrome. Believe me, you don't want to go there. Pacing yourself, especially after what may be a more justifiable early sprint to get started, will likely feel counterintuitive. But there is plenty of research showing the lack of correlation between hours worked and productivity. In fact, some studies show an inverse correlation. The Organization for Economic Cooperation and Development (OECD) has tracked this for many years, by country. Among developed economies, for example, Ireland has nearly three times more productivity per worker than does South Korea—yet Koreans work 11 percent more hours than the Irish. Ireland's average work week (hours actually worked) is three hours shorter than America's. (The U.S. ranks only seventh among OECD countries in GDP per hour worked; I suppose I share the blame with all those excess hours I used to put in.) So if you're starting your independent journey with the belief that more hours dependably equals more productivity, change your mind. (That said, "nothing to excess" also includes loafing.)

The cherry on top is happiness. When we overlay data from the OECD and the annual World Happiness Report (published by the Sustainable Development Solutions Network and based on Gallup and Lloyd's surveys), we see that the three happiest among the OECD's 37 member countries—#1 Finland, #2 Denmark, and #3 Norway—work 7, 16, and 15 percent fewer hours, respectively, than the 37-country average. Of course it's harder to be happy in bad health, and a recent World Health Organization study estimates that overwork kills three quarters of a million people a year. It also showed correlation between working more than 55 hours a week and increased risk of stroke and heart disease. So much for my wish to maintain some level of lightheartedness in this book.

Resting can take many forms. It certainly transcends number of hours worked or not worked. Most basic is sleep. Don't let Thomas Edison fool you with his average of three to four hours of sleep. Sleep is a consummate trickster, perpetually tempting us with simple math: fewer hours slept equals getting more stuff done, right? And cheating the seven hours (or even eight as more sleep experts now recommend) that your body and mind probably want will more than likely sabotage you in both seen and unseen ways. Sleep deprivation or insufficiency, so common among entrepreneurs, manifests in more wide-ranging ways than most people think. It not only compromises focus and concentration, memory, and mood, but also physical resilience—weakening your immune system and ability to cope with stress, increasing risk of diabetes, heart disease, and high blood pressure, while also diminishing coordination. And that's just the physical parts, which can challenge relationships too.

The other trickster aspect of sleep is that research shows how workaholism in the very early stages actually produces pleasing and positive emotions, with minimal adverse consequences. So this can be quite addictive until those consequences ratchet up. And they will, without proper rest. Be extremely vigilant, especially in those first years, in monitoring whether you're truly getting enough rest.

The next best thing to sleep is taking enough breaks. Depending on the nature of your work, pauses can save your health (or even your life; that's why European truck drivers are required to take 45-minute breaks every 4-1/2 hours). Remember the hourly chime app on my smartphone that I mentioned in Chapter 5? I also use it to remind me to take breaks. When I was in the thick of the early days of my business, pre-smartphones, by the time I realized I was getting bleary-eyed I would have already skipped another meal or forgotten to exercise.

Even something as simple as listening to music during a break can relax and restore you, and can even inform the work when you return to it. I've been amazed to find, beyond relaxation, ideas and inspiration in micro doses of music—be it the introspection and soul-searching of singer/songwriters, the improvisation of jazz, the soulfulness of R&B, the stories of country music, the hard truths of hip-hop, the emotional catharsis of opera, or the precision of a great orchestra. All music has the capacity to inspire imagination and incite self-examination—two important gateways to a happier work life.

Finally, a reminder: I can't overstate that a very important complementary preventer of No Boss burnout is getting the help you need (remember Lesson 6 and review as needed!). Effectively done, it can be the difference in whether you have adequate time to rest.

## Mindfulness

Another complementary preventer of No Boss burnout is mindfulness. Three mindful things have helped me enormously in coping with the slings and arrows of self-employment: conquering worry (I'm still working on that), meditation, and walking in fresh outdoor air.

Test the utility of worrying. In the movie "Bridge of Spies," when Tom Hanks is defending a Soviet spy arrested in America, twice during the movie Hanks asks the spy why he didn't seem worried about his impending trial and sentencing. Both times the spy replied, "Would it help?" He had a point. If I had a dollar for every minute I spent worrying about my business, I wouldn't have needed to *have* a business. Did it help? Can you honestly think of an instance when it really helped *you*? (Don't confuse worrying with planning.)

But something that did help was a counterpoint to worrying: meditation. The mindfulness that comes with meditation has been a wonderful aid in staying in the present rather than regretting past actions or fearing the future—two places where our brains spend far too much time. Destructive time. In the midst of my busiest days, even a brief meditation of ten minutes refreshes, clears my head, and allows me to be more present and productive afterwards.

In the first half of my consulting career, meeting with mostly Silicon Valley clients, I would arrive at my client company's parking lot 15 minutes early and use that time for last-minute "cramming" to review my notes. In later years, even if I thought a meeting's outcome was really important to my finances, I instead used that same time to meditate in the car, do a bit of deep breathing, try to detach from outcome, and calmly walk into the lobby.

I have no doubt that my independent work has benefitted, and far beyond just meetings. There are too many good books on meditation to delve into technique here, but I encourage you to explore them if you're not already meditating. Worrying doesn't help, but meditation does—and truly can be a powerful way to mitigate worry and serve as an antidote for the stresses of self-employment.

And then there is walking. Henry David Thoreau had the right idea. His famous essay from the 1850's, "Walking," heightened awareness of the salutary effects of the outdoors on mind and body. ("Will not man grow to greater perfection intellectually as well as physically under these influences?") Yet walking need not be in the woods or the wild. I seldom have had time on busy days to walk anywhere beyond my neighborhood. I do take issue with one thing Thoreau said about walking: "What business have I in the woods, if I am thinking of something other than the woods?" The fact is, some of my best ideas have come to me while walking and letting the mind wander.

So you need not feel like you're neglecting your independent work while walking. Or meditating. You're *nourishing* it.

## Consciousness

Consciousness and mindfulness are not the same thing. When building and nurturing an independent business, its potentially all-consuming nature can back us into a narrow corridor of focus that squeezes out our peripheral vision of life. Especially if you're operating as essentially a one-person business, you can wake up one day and realize you've been in a self-absorbed "it's all about me" groove—the daily obsession with what's good for me and what's good for my business. But it's good business to be in touch, and stay in touch, with the greater good. A concept from the corporate world (of all places!), "the purpose-driven enterprise," helps explain why. Deliberateness and consciousness of purpose (beyond earning money), besides being good for its beneficiaries, drive meaning and satisfaction and can also create otherwise unseen business opportunities.

"Purpose-driven" has gained great momentum in just the last few years among companies of all sizes, but especially among larger publicly traded companies—not just because they are under increasing scrutiny by all stakeholders (employees, customers, investors, suppliers, regulators), but because it's also proving to be good business. In contrast to decades of doctrine that companies exist for the sole purpose of creating value for their shareholders, we have clearly entered an era in which the most successful businesses believe they have a greater purpose than returning a handsome profit on their stock. These companies have significantly broadened and deepened their answer to "why we exist." Tesla is in business "to accelerate the planet's transition to sustainable energy"; Apple to "create tools for the mind to advance humankind"; Chobani to "make better food for more people"; REI to "awaken a lifelong love of the outdoors." It's easy to be cynical about mission statements that sound like slogans, since so many companies have talked the talk without walking the walk. But for the ones that walk, the rewards are great: the global consultancy Deloitte reports that truly purpose-driven companies are growing three times faster than their competitors, simultaneously increasing market share, customer satisfaction, and workforce satisfaction.

There is no reason why consciousness and being purpose-driven can't convey the same benefits to an independent business, no matter how small. Twelve years ago, I added a sustainability component (specifically, environmental impact) to software I had designed for optimizing product development decisions. This reinvigorated my relationship with my work, knowing that I might now have a tool to help convince companies to design more environmentally friendly products. At that time I didn't think about how being more purpose-driven would open up other opportunities both rich in meaning and good for my business. But it led to being invited to speak at major conferences on sustainable business practices and to become a contributing writer for two prominent online portals for sustainable business ideas and information.

So think deeply about why your No Boss business will exist (or already does) beyond earning a livelihood and feeling productive. Purpose beyond profit is a win-win for your psychological well-being and your business outcomes, and will help sustain you for the long haul.

## Gratitude

Self-employment is a privilege, especially in developed economies. This bears repeating: self-employment is a *privilege*. That's too easy to forget on your worst days, when it may feel more like punishment. But the No Boss community is indeed a select group. According to the International Labor Organization, less than 10-15 percent of people in developed economies are self-employed. Yet a recent Dartmouth College survey found that a (shocking?) 70 percent of full-time employeds would prefer to be self-employed. The overwhelming majority of people in first-world countries are being bossed around by someone they have no control over. Be thankful for having some control over how you do that to yourself.

Gratitude is not just touchy-feely positive thinking. Studies analyzed by the University of California–Berkeley's Greater Good Science Center have shown important links between gratitude and performance. Gratitude practice helps people transition out of stressful states into greater relaxation, increases sleep quality, reduces inflammation, and boosts optimism. Some high-performance people keep a gratitude journal. I've found it helpful to make a daily practice of silently enumerating at least three to five things I'm grateful for. (It's also a nice way to end meditation.) Those gratitudes have often included something about work, like the flexibility that I have in managing my time, or being able to scale back my workload in "retirement years" without actually retiring when I still want to serve clients but with a lighter load. But they also include really important things outside of work made possible by that flexibility—like restoring my energy and creativity through other pursuits, or time with family and friends. Staying connected to gratitude each day, however you incorporate it as a practice, makes you more resilient in the face of business challenges, unpleasant surprises, bad days, and disappointments—all of which are inevitable. That resilience, combined with a feeling of privilege, can really help power you through difficult moments and longer difficult periods.

## Grace and the Long Haul

Though "long haul" is a 150-year-old phrase that came from the railroads, it's part of the title of this chapter because its dictionary definition is so relevant to sustaining an independent business for many years: "something that takes a long time and a lot of effort." But you can do it gracefully with the support of resting, mindfulness, consciousness, and gratitude—a powerful cocktail for anyone's well-being, but especially anyone sustaining an independent business for many years.

With that grace and well-being, No Boss flexibility also provides a gateway to a larger life. We explore that next.

\* \* \*

LESSON 11

# Independent Work as a Gateway to a Larger Life

*"You have to color outside the lines once in a while if you want to make your life a masterpiece."*
~ Albert Einstein

*"A mind that is stretched by new experiences can never go back to its old dimensions."*
~ Oliver Wendell Holmes Sr.

What good is all your newfound flexibility if it isn't leveraged into a broader, richer life adventure beyond work? If you thought your dreams beyond work were constrained by the confines of toiling away for someone else, don't think that can't happen in self-employment. But if you're vigilant about workaholism and the sustaining strategies in Lesson 10, chances are good that independent flexibility can translate to painting your life on a bigger canvas with richer colors.

My first decade of self-employment was preceded by five years of working for companies, and followed by five more years of doing the same (to get more experience on the "client side" of consulting). In those latter five years, I noticed that my life was contracting as I took on more and more responsibility. It became all about the office. But within a couple of years after subsequently returning to independent work, and even with intense focus on building a consulting practice and taking good care of clients, I noticed that two things were happening that seemed impossible when I was employed. I had started work on my second book, and had also taken my guitar out of closet storage and begun writing songs again. Both of those activities obviously took time, but they also nourished me with energy and fresh perspectives for problem-solving in my business. I'm convinced to this day that it was that particular energy that allowed me to create the Strategic Harmony® decision model for my client companies to use to their advantage. My independent work benefitted rather than suffered.

Using different parts of your brain than you use in your business each day, and flexing different creative muscles, also serve as insurance against business burnout. They refresh the mind and contribute to physical well-being. University of Pennsylvania professor Philip Tetlock's research even showed how specialization in a single-minded endeavor can detract from good judgment. Being too exclusively focused on work can make you what novelist E.M. Forster called one-dimensional characters: he dubbed them "flat people," in contrast to "rounded people." Who wants to be a flat person? What happens when you turn sideways?

## Liberating the Polymath in All of Us

The English word *polymath* first surfaced in the early 1600's, derived from the Greek *polumathēs*—"having learned much." In contemporary English it describes a person of broad knowledge and abilities. There is a polymath in all of us that's begging to burst free, and self-employed flexibility can often be its ticket out.

As polymath Waqās Ahmed, artist/neuroscientist/journalist and book author, wrote, "We are all born with an innate disposition that is curious, creative, and versatile." That versatility and curiosity can be severely constrained or even snuffed out by work-life imbalance that is too often a consequence of specialized employment. Pursuing some other interest(s) is an antidote that No Boss flexibility can promote. But only if you use it.

I'm not suggesting that being your own boss means needing to become Leonardo da Vinci, the quintessential polymath (excelling with monumental talent and deep knowledge across architecture, engineering, sculpture, painting, mathematics, and multiple scientific fields ranging from anatomy to zoology). I'm not even suggesting that you become a master of one other field besides your core area of livelihood, like self-employed insurance agent/composer Charles Ives (who is credited with important innovative firsts in the insurance industry while composing some of the most innovative works of American classical music), or like pediatrician-obstetrician and famed poet William Carlos Williams (who wrote enduring poetry on prescription pads in between patients and delivering more than 3,000 babies). But we can learn from these masters without having to be one.

In his early thirties, Charles Ives left his insurance company job to set out on his own. He simultaneously pursued building an independent business and pushing the boundaries of classical music composition. If it had not been his music that won him a Pulitzer Prize and landed his face on a U.S. postage stamp, his achievements as a self-employed independent insurance agent throughout his most productive years as a composer would still have brought him acclaim in the business world. He pioneered the concept of estate planning, and created a training program for insurance agents that was adopted by almost every large insurance company. His business ultimately became the largest insurance agency in America. But always as a businessman, Ives believed that art is a natural part of being human. Art can push one to break molds. Breaking molds in business helps you stand out from your competition, just as it did for Ives. He looked forward to a day when (in his early 20th-century parlance) "every man, while digging his potatoes, will breathe his own epics, his own symphonies." He even wrote a song about business ("Ann Street"). Biographer Sidney Cowell put it well: "The period of Ives's most strenuous devotion to his business was also the period of his most energetic creative production of music. He was no split personality, but functioned as the same whole man wherever you find him, with a fine flow of creative energy that crystallized and organized business ideas into new relationships just as it did his musical ideas at home in the evening."

Similarly, William Carlos Williams integrated his two pursuits to the advantage of both. In his autobiography he said, "As a writer, I have been a physician, and as a physician I have been a writer." He went on to say that he treated his patients as works of art. (I wish some of my doctors had treated me that way!) At the end of a particularly difficult workday for a doctor holding someone's life in his hands, he described his art as a "cleansing of the day's torment." That had to be good for his next workday.

Ah, you say, but that was a different era. Doesn't matter: today there are untold numbers of contemporary examples living among us that confirm the mutually reinforcing rewards of non-singular pursuits. Silicon Valley investor Roger McNamee still finds time to play in a rock band that tours and plays music festivals and clubs. He has described how that puts him in small towns around the country, staying in modest motels, which in turn keeps him in touch with Main Street concerns that inform his investment decisions and knowledge of what products and services the mass market wants. This has undoubtedly been a factor in his outsized business success and personal wealth, and an advantage versus rival investors who seldom leave their Silicon Valley perches except for business trips replete with posh hotels and fine restaurants. Chicago public relations consultant Michelle Mekky talks about how boxing has made her more successful in business, improving her focus and mind-over-matter determination. Entrepreneur Richard Branson's self-employment journey from first startup to owning more than 200 businesses did not prevent him from pursuing his passion for flight while still in his thirties; in fact, his crossings of both the Atlantic and Pacific Oceans in a hot air balloon provoked great publicity that, in his words, "helped put Virgin [Virgin Atlantic Airways] on the map." Some may say that it's easy for wealthy celebrities to pursue other passions. But for every celebrity story like Branson's there are countless others among self-employed people who walk among us and whose names we do not know. At least not yet.

So, clearly, we need not become as accomplished in multiple pursuits at the level of an Ives or a Williams to enjoy more fulfillment and a larger life than our work alone can provide. Nor do we need to have full-fledged dual careers. Nor do 'non-work' pursuits need to be in the arts. However we do it, we can all avoid the trap of independent workaholism by giving into other productive urges, be they creative, academic, athletic, focused on the natural world, or in any field of interest, learning, or self-expression. Regardless, if Ives or Williams were still with us, they would tell you—as would so many of their contemporary descendants with dual or multiple pursuits—that there is more evidence of synergy between their endeavors than sacrifice of either. I deeply believe it, having personally found it to be the case over and over again.

In Lesson 2 I said that authenticity can take you far in independent work (or any work, for that matter). People sense when you are your authentic self; there's such power in that! If you have a deep passion beyond work that you're not pursuing, I think of that as a form of denying your authenticity. In your independence resides the gift of time, even when you think you don't have it. Self-employed psychiatrist Denny Zeitlin, during decades of seeing patients in full-time private practice, found time to record more than 100 original compositions as a jazz pianist and perform solo at Carnegie Hall to rave reviews. The point is not to miss the opportunity to in some way leverage No Boss flexibility into a richer tapestry of life, which can also energize your independent business in mysterious and wonderful ways.

## Giving Back

Stepping out on your own is inherently a self-centered endeavor, especially in the early going. It can require so much of you that helping others may not even be on your radar for quite a long time. Understandable for sure. I'm reluctant to admit that I was already midway through my No Boss journey before I undertook any serious *pro bono* work. When I finally did, working with the Sightline Institute, an environmental policy think tank that has accomplished great things, the satisfaction was perhaps predictable—but the energy

I derived from it was a surprise. Just as polymathic pursuits can be a source of creative ideas and energy for your independent business, so can giving back. Norman Vincent Peale, often called the father of positive thinking, was really onto something when he said that the act of giving is a *personal power-releasing* factor.

It may seem that independent work would make it harder to give back. After all, there's usually not a lot of extra cash for sizable donations, especially early on, and no one to cover for you when you're not working. More and more forward-thinking companies do provide for and encourage volunteer work on company time. However, many opportunities to volunteer or do pro bono work require committing to daytime hours that conflict with employment. There, independent flexibility strikes again.

I've been greatly nourished by such opportunities that were only possible because of my No Boss flexibility. Some of the contacts I've made this way have also been very good for my business. For example, the pro bono work with Sightline heightened my awareness of environmental issues in ways that informed my decision to integrate environmental impact metrics into the Strategic Harmony® model and software I mentioned earlier. That became another differentiator for my business. Likewise, serving on an advisory committee for my city government, which works to attract entrepreneurs to the city, has given me insights into what kinds of programs can help independent businesses flourish. It also provided local networking opportunities.

The win-win of giving back never goes out of style. Even Charles Ives during World War II, when his health excluded him from enlisting in the military, donated the money for an ambulance and offered to drive it for six months. Character and integrity attract people; you never know how it may also attract clients or customers, partners or employees, or other people important to your independent business. While that shouldn't be a motive for giving back, there's nothing wrong with accepting any good fortune that giving happens to bring. In any case, there will be joy.

\* \* \*

# LESSON 12

♦

## Lessons from Others

♦

*"Your assumptions are your windows on the world.
Scrub them off every once in a while, or the light won't come in."*
~ Isaac Asimov

*"Learn every day, but especially from the experiences of others.
It's cheaper!"*
~ John Bogle

One of the great comforts of independent work has been relationships with others who are also on the No Boss journey. Successful self-employeds are among the very smartest people I've had the good fortune to know. I've learned much from them, and mutual sharing of experiences has been very satisfying.

What you've read up to this point is essentially one person's perspective, so I asked some of the most thoughtful and interesting people in my self-employed network to reflect on being their own boss—and then to weigh in on seven questions inextricably tied to the themes of this book. This cohort of successful people with diverse backgrounds and interests spans the fields of business consulting, technical consulting, graphic arts, journalism, medicine, law, psychotherapy, physical therapy, executive coaching, life coaching, and even a chef with a one-man (so far) bottled sauce business. All of these respondents are productively self-employed, with years of triumphs and scars to prove it. And they previously worked for companies earlier in their careers, so they are veterans of being bossed around by others before bossing themselves around.

For those of you concerned about hearing from only a sample of one (me), the good news (for me too) is that the preceding eleven lessons have been largely echoed by these No Boss compatriots. But these wise adventurers also put additional color on those issues, and raised a few new ones as well. I share highlights of their insights with you now.

First, the seven questions:

1. Looking back to when you left your last job, what was the biggest factor in your decision to be your own boss?
2. For you, what's been the best thing about working independently?
3. What's been the worst?
4. What's been the biggest surprise relative to your initial expectations?
5. What have you missed most (excluding steady paychecks) about no longer being employed by someone else?
6. What's the first piece of advice you would give someone (currently and previously employed by others) who is contemplating being their own boss?
7. What advice would you have for newly self-employeds to sustain success over the long haul?

For each question's responses, I looked for patterns while paying attention to what was similar to or different from my own experience. Here are those themes, peppered with verbatim excerpts (italicized in quotes) from my committee of experts, along with my commentary.

## 1. What was the biggest factor in your decision to be your own boss?

This is the hardest question to find patterns on, as it's such an individualized personal decision made in widely varying circumstances. But think about to what degree you see yourself in any or all of the themes below, as my respondents have experienced some meaningful level of these things through independent work (yes, it's doable!). Those themes:

- Control over my destiny
- Wanting to succeed or fail on my own terms, rather than through the efforts or missteps of others
- The desire to create something from scratch
- Belief in having a better way to do something than currently available solutions
- Never finding a job that was the best fit for my strengths, and a deep desire to maximize the use of those strengths
- Control over work-life balance
- Family considerations (e.g., more time with my kids, or last child going away to college creating more flexibility for a parent)
- Escaping from company politics
- Needing a new challenge

A few also cited exhaustion from employment. But I don't recommend exhaustion as a great incentive to start an independent business. You may well work harder than you've ever worked.

Also recall what I said at the beginning of Lesson 2 about the importance of running *toward* something rather than running *away* from something. Most of the themes above are running toward something positive. *Escape*, however, whether from exhaustion, company politics, or anything negative, *is not a strategy for independent business success.*

Here is a response from a highly respected doctor who, when employed early in his career, experienced constraints that caused him to doubt if he even still wanted to be a doctor. He then started and maintained a very successful solo practice completely outside the insurance system—very hard to do, but utter independence for all the right reasons. *"As my own boss I could fashion my medical practice … the way that I believed could help my patients make the kind of progress they had been unable to make in the conventional model. I could spend two or three hours with a new patient and begin the process of developing a relationship … developing trust and respect required for any successful partnership. Having the time to get to know patients has led to more accurate diagnoses, more effective treatments, and teaching patients self-care skills. In these ways and more I could be happy being a doctor."*

Another recurring theme was self-confidence—a belief that the potential for one's capabilities to shine brighter without the shackles of employment outweighed the support that the structure (and infrastructure) of employment provides. As one consultant put it, having been employed for 25 years before setting out on his own, *"I had self-confidence in my ability to make high-value contributions to companies struggling with growth … without all the politics, empire building, and inertia issues that internal change agents have to contend with. Doing what's right for the business … requires having the freedom to say what I think … and do what you do best."*

Then there is the issue of aligning work with your values. Even as companies become more purpose-driven, some people have found it difficult to find employers who inspire them with a socially positive mission and actions and can also make the best use of their skills. As an attorney said when asked for reasons he decided on a solo practice: *"The desire to maximize the extent to which I could autonomously fashion my work life to fit my ideas about societal usefulness. This required maximizing control over the issues involved in the cases that I would accept, the number and type of clients who I would represent, my fee structure (including flexibility to serve other practice goals), and the approach I took to representation."*

Also mentioned by a journalist was the desire for more control over the physical work environment for health reasons. If you happen to be a person with sensitivities to chemicals, building products, or poor indoor air, self-employed work from home can be your ticket to a healthier workplace.

Noteworthy is that not a single respondent mentioned "to make more money" as their motive for being their own boss. I don't think it's an accident that most of my respondents are successful, as money is better thought of as an outcome rather than a primary motivation (especially if employment has been meeting your basic financial needs up to the point of your decision).

## 2. What's been the best thing about working independently?

Themes:

- Being personally responsible for outcomes
- Work has felt more meaningful
- Enjoying figuring things out on my own
- Choosing the people I work with (and who I don't!)
- Control over time—both within work hours and allocation to other things
- Flexibility to more easily attend to family needs as necessary
- Continuous learning
- No one telling me what to do—or telling me how to do it when I believe I have a better way
- Not feeling trapped in negative workplace dynamics
- Allows me to be the best that I can be

Not surprising that *control* is a prevalent theme among the best things about working independently—control over who you work with, and how you allocate your time. Isn't control the essence of No Boss?

But with that control come new depths of responsibility. And yet this responsibility also surfaced as one of the best things about independent work. The recurring theme of taking personal responsibility for outcomes goes hand in hand with what we heard in Question 1 about self-confidence. Successful self-employeds embrace *owning* the results, good or bad, of their efforts. As one of my respondents succinctly put it, *"Whether or not things go well comes down to me."*

While it may seem that there's a kind of perversity in wanting to really own failures and not just successes, my experience has been that failing all on your own is the purest form of constructive learning (vs. failing as part of a team). When I have failed to win a consulting engagement that I competed for alone, I didn't have to wonder if that was because of someone else's actions. With no team there is no one to scapegoat. I could instead focus on what I could have done better and apply it next time, and reflect on it once again during my Lesson 8 performance reviews. Working independently removes a huge amount of the noise when thinking about why something did or didn't work out.

Control over who you work with came up often, but can even be more important if you're an introvert. It's not just about the quiet. We've all been thrust into situations where we have to work with people who we would just as soon have never even met. As one of my respondents said, *"The best thing is the lack of workplace drama. It is such a relief not to have to deal with the problems that arise interpersonally in the workplace."*

An interesting twist on responsibility came from more than one respondent (and is echoed by me as well): if you provide an advisory service like consulting or coaching, and were formerly employed as a manager or executive, there is actually great relief in—as one coach put it—no longer being the one who is actually doing the heavy lifting. (Not unlike American football, where the quarterback takes the bruising hits of 260-pound tackles while the coach stands on the sidelines after calling the plays.) So this relief can be one of the best things about independent advisory work as a counterbalance to the full weight of responsibility for No Boss success.

We not only learn a great deal about ourselves from failures, but also from the people that are helped by our work. As a legendary executive coach responding to Question 2 said, *"I really appreciate the diversity of clients I got to work with and how much I learned about myself in the process of coaching hundreds of managers."* And then there is the broader continuous learning when working outside the bounds of being employed by one company. Advising more than 50 companies has taught me so much about so many businesses, so many management styles, and what improves or impedes results that I couldn't have possibly learned within the confines of one or even a handful of employers.

Just as my fellow self-employeds embraced the fullness of responsibility, some (more than others) also very much embraced the uncertainty. As a counterpoint to what can be a lonely No Boss existence, the intense and quiet journey of figuring things out on your own and converting ambiguity to certitude can be immensely satisfying. As a respondent who is a business development advisor in healthcare technology said, *"I like the adrenaline and challenge of being up against it where it's not obvious which direction to take or even which task to complete next."*

Then there is the matter of stage of life. Respondents in their child-raising years especially value the flexibility of independent work, but so do those in the latter stages of their work life. As another executive coach said, *"At this stage of life and career, there are additional personal interests as well as activities to give back that are important to me to devote time toward. Having my own business allows me to directly control the amount of time I allocate to work and other areas."*

The points I've commented on here all feed the overall sense of increased meaningfulness that respondents reported when reflecting on the best things about independent work.

## 3. What's been the worst thing about working independently?

Themes (take heed!):

- Feelings of isolation and loneliness
- Perfectionism has made me a punishing boss of myself
- The instability of the first few years, and the lack of financial resources especially in the earliest stages
- An ongoing struggle to set boundaries around work
- Marketing myself, and deciding how much time and resources to put against that
- The administrative part, and the tax complications vs. being employed

The sunniest response to this question came from a respondent who said that the worst thing about working independently has been "Nothing—absolutely no downside." Nice to hear from someone I know to be an honest person. But the themes above, as well as my many confessions during the course of this book, betray the fact that she has been exceptionally lucky or has an unusual capacity to forget negative experiences.

Regarding isolation and loneliness, Lesson 6 already covered how getting the help you need can mitigate those feelings. As one of my respondents said, it's been easier to address that issue than addressing being under-resourced. But another respondent admitted that years of working alone has almost broken her spirit at times, missing being part of a work community even while acknowledging the inevitable problems with that. Independence can be particularly hard on extroverts, who thrive on people interaction. On the other hand, introverts get re-energized by time alone. So where you sit on the introvert-extrovert continuum can be a partial predictor of how you will fare in these feelings.

Then there is the struggle to set boundaries, which has many facets. One is purely about the number of hours worked. One of my respondents, a leadership trainer and workshop facilitator, even proclaimed that *"You'll work one third more than when you worked for a company."* (And she had had big jobs in big companies.) But releasing on perfectionism, also among the themes above, will help reduce those hours. The nature of the work also makes boundaries easier or harder, depending on the degree to which you need to be "on call." For example, a freelance editor talked about never knowing at any hour when an email will arrive that requires immediate initiation of a project.

The boundaries theme certainly intersects with the "punishing boss" theme. The irony of self-employment control was well captured by this comment: *"I have worked harder than perhaps I needed to, cared more than perhaps I should have, come home late too many nights, and cut out too many lunches. This is someone who is making his own schedule? Go figure."*

Most everyone cited, often joylessly, the need to market ourselves. It comes naturally to some, but not to most—even those of us who know a lot about marketing. For the majority of my respondents it was their least favorite thing. Some pointed out the workflow challenge of keeping their pipelines filled with upcoming projects while trying to focus on managing current projects. Others simply don't like selling themselves and just want to do the work (certainly the case with me). Others, especially early in their journey, were bewildered by the array of marketing options and how to allocate their marketing time. As one said: *"There is an almost limitless number of things that one can do to build awareness and generate business opportunities (networking, postings, articles, conferences, certifications, etc.). Determining the optimal amount of time to devote to these, and what activities are the most value-added, can be difficult to ascertain."* Others acknowledged the need to engage a social media expert. But a technical consultant pointed out a silver lining in self-marketing besides the obvious sales outcomes: *"The need to market myself motivated me to attend industry functions and participate in volunteer committees that have made a positive difference in my professional community."* Meaningfulness comes in many forms, including outside one's comfort zone.

## 4. What's been the biggest surprise relative to your initial expectations?

Themes:

- Increased productivity
- Exceeding my income expectations
- Support from friends and business contacts
- Becoming more well-rounded, by necessity
- Humility, from finding out what's required to run your own business

Beyond the desire to work independently, before taking the plunge many had questioned whether they had the self-discipline to work alone or from home—and have been pleasantly surprised by accomplishing more in less time. In Lesson 5 I covered the outsized role of keeping perfectionism at bay to boost productivity. Yes, there are distractions at home, as even those of you still employed may have experienced during Covid. But there can also be plenty of distractions in the workplace—from unnecessary (and unnecessarily long) meetings to ineffectual team dynamics to bureaucratic administrative time sinks.

Hand in hand with pleasant surprises on productivity have been pleasant surprises on income. Even a few of my most confident and experienced respondents have been astounded at the businesses they've built mostly by themselves. There are two asterisks on that. First, if you're selling a physical product rather than a service, there is a greater likelihood that things go slower than expected. You're more dependent on a supply chain and other uncontrollables. Second, when you're working independently for the long haul in any business, there are bound to be those difficult macroeconomic periods. If you're a consultant of any kind, you may be the first to go in a recession when companies tighten their belts. But the people I know who are committed to independent work have weathered these storms, becoming more recession-proof by adjusting their pricing or making themselves indispensable (my favorite strategy!).

Some even got started when the Great Recession triggered mass layoffs and companies needed to contract independent expertise to temporarily fill holes in their organization.

Several respondents have been buoyed by the surprise of how many people have been willing to help them, primarily with referrals. But we all know that doesn't just happen without past and ongoing efforts on your part to build and maintain relationships. As one consultant said, *"I was surprised by how willing my friends and business school classmates are to send business my way. Business development has turned out to be very personal for me—with the most effective efforts being simply staying in touch, maintaining friendships and acquaintances, and being transparent (and very low-key) about the ongoing need to sell work."* Relationships *within* one's independent business has also been a surprise to some: *"A great surprise has been the quality of the relationships I've had with clients … very different than what I'd experienced as a one-time commissioned salesperson."* And if you're in a service business, the fact that employed clients change jobs more often than ever before makes those relationships even more important—as they will "take you with them" when they move if they truly value your work.

Then there was the well-roundedness theme, which surfaced as a surprise on two important dimensions. First is the jack-of-all-trades aspect, captured by this respondent: *"There were many things that initially I thought I could never do, but I surprised myself multiple times by figuring them out on my own—and that is a gratifying feeling. When I was employed in an office, there was always an IT person on hand to take care of computer problems or help me learn new software. But I had to figure all this stuff out for myself. Even more important than figuring things out was learning how to figure things out. It's both a skill and a mindset, and it has proven invaluable for self-employment, as well as life in general. When there is no one to answer your questions, you learn how to be resourceful."*

The second aspect of well-roundedness isn't always a positive, as framed by this career coach who had previously been very successfully employed for decades: *"Despite many years of professional experience and exposure to a wide variety of industries, functional disciplines, and company environments, it has been humbling to recognize how much I didn't know about various aspects of running my own business."* That's a huge part of "figuring things out." But the No Boss journey is sink or swim, and most of us figure out how to swim—especially if we're a generally good fit for independent work (Lesson 4). Otherwise, you could find yourself trying to swim in quicksand.

## 5. What have you missed most (excluding steady paychecks) about no longer being employed by someone else?

Themes:

- Collaboration and camaraderie
- Resources
- Infrastructure
- Opportunities for growth unique to employment
- Company benefits
- The commute (yes, really—for some)

Missing collaboration and the camaraderie of the workplace is the flip side of the isolation and loneliness that came up in responses to Question 3. Well summarized by one respondent after many years employed by large companies, *"This includes learning from, and being challenged by, colleagues as well as the social connections. Additionally, as a sole practitioner it is more challenging to find opportunities to bounce ideas off of others, obtain constructive feedback, and simply have someone to brainstorm with."* Others mentioned the team spirit of working in groups, as well as the *fun*. The importance of fun can't be overstated as counterweight to the demands of successful independent work. But I would also remind us that there are plenty of different kinds of fun to be had in an independent business if it's a good fit for you, and you can also get some of that collaborative stimulation and fun if your business is conducive to partnering (Lesson 7). Regardless, you're creating a business even if you're not creating an invention per se and, as Einstein said, "Creativity is intelligence having fun." Sure feels like it.

Two other themes—missing the resources of employment and the infrastructure of employment—are closely related. Just as an employer's people and money help you get things done, so does the workplace (and remote) infrastructure that employers provide. If only I had a dollar for the thousands of minutes I've burned in being my own IT Department. We already saw in the responses to Question 3 the expressions of frustration at being under-resourced for building a business. Nothing was starker for me than going from managing a $70 million budget in a big company in the early 1990's (more than $130 million in today's dollars) to suddenly having to write personal checks for everything work-related, from supplies to travel. So be sure you have the stomach for it if you're used to being reasonably resourced. Had I not been my own boss earlier in my career, I can't be sure I would have been scrappy enough.

Regarding opportunities for growth afforded by employment, chief among them is the ongoing chance to learn from more experienced colleagues or even be actively mentored by one or more of them—especially if you're on the younger side. More and more companies have embraced employee rotation as a human resources strategy, broadening skillsets and experience by moving people into different jobs each year or even every few months over some period of time. Other employment opportunities may include paid-for special training, education, certifications, and networking among peers and leaders in other companies. I owe some of my own professional growth to employers who sent me to Harvard Business School for post-graduate executive education, and to out-of-town industry conferences that I couldn't have justified paying for on my own.

Of course other company benefits have been greatly missed. My respondents called out the obvious but they bear repeating: health insurance (for my American respondents) and dental and vision coverage, paid vacation time, paid sick leave, and in some cases paid time off for community service.

It may surprise you that some of my No Boss compatriots actually also missed their commute after leaving their jobs. (So did fully one third of employeds who had to work from home during Covid, according to a survey by Randstad, the U.K. talent recruiting firm.) Some just preferred to get out of their house or apartment every day. But as one of my respondents explained, *"I miss the forced regular periods of decompression listening to music or just being quiet and thinking while driving to and from an office."* So did I in terms of having transition time in between the stress of work and time with family back in the days when I had a long commute. That's a polite way of saying that I was less likely to arrive home in a hellacious mood and take it out on my wife and toddler. Sometimes as my own boss later on, but when I still had a child at home, being with family just two minutes after abruptly ending my workday was like whiplash without that transition time—no matter how happy I was to see them.

Finally, my respondents' (and my own) missing the steady paycheck was mitigated by two things. First, time. As your No Boss income stream starts to build and startup expenses wane, the initial big gulp when no employer's direct deposit arrives in your bank account will fade. Second, respondents acknowledge that job security isn't what it once was and these days is often a mirage. As one quipped, *"Job security is great until they decide to let you go."* Another: *"If I'm going to be insecure in employment, I figured I might as well go out and do that on my own."* Even before Covid, job security had been continuously declining for the past few decades due to global competition, economic crises, and employers' desire for more workforce flexibility. Everyone missed that paycheck at first. But we all just had to keep reminding ourselves that we didn't miss bad bosses, the lack of control, bureaucracy, or workplace politics. Still, know what you're giving up when you're the boss, which was the point of Question 5.

## 6. What's the first piece of advice you would give someone (currently and previously employed by others) who is contemplating being their own boss?

Themes:

- Ask yourself (and other trusted people) the hard questions about *you*
- Resist the naysayers
- Differentiate
- Charge what you're worth
- Get it in writing
- Be prepared for success taking longer
- Protect your health and your personal relationships

The first advice to you from nearly all my respondents echoed the central theme of Lesson 4—confronting who you really are to determine if independent work is a good fit for you. A very successful leadership consultant framed some pointed questions this way: *"How important is it to you to have performance expectations set by others? Can you imagine getting up every morning and working, even though no one is telling you that you have to? Is it enough for you to know you're doing a great job, or do you need to hear it? How important is it for you to have colleagues with whom you can brainstorm and problem solve (or, complain!)? How do you usually deal with risk? Failure?"*

Beyond thoughtfully answering such questions for yourself, respondents also stressed the importance of reaching out for objective feedback. As one said, *"Make sure you have the know-how and soft skills to get your idea off the ground. Confirm with a competent friend who is willing to be direct and truthful with you."* Going a step further: *"Look for an opportunity to launch a business that someone else wants to see launched. Get them to back you."*

Another advice theme: resist the naysayers when you start telling people you plan to be, or are even thinking about, stepping out on your own. From a technical consultant on government projects who has sustained a successful business for decades: *"Try to ignore all your co-workers, family, and friends (and internal negative voices in your own head) that tell you it's too risky to go out on your own. If I had listened to them, I would've never gone out of my comfort zone."*

He also echoed other respondents in underscoring the importance of differentiation. So many independent businesses fail because, as he put it, *"Just saying you do great software development or fantastic document editing doesn't differentiate you from the crowd. How are you better? How will you make them sleep better at night?"* If you're not bringing a new idea to market (which by definition suggests that you're first), dig deep to articulate what makes you different and why prospective clients/customers should care. Another respondent who helps senior executives prepare for job interviews reminded us that, especially in a service business, to effectively market yourself it's just as important to understand what differentiates you personally and not just your service or business: *"Discover your differentiating qualities—deeply ingrained ones that have been apparent your whole life. (What kinds of things have every group you worked or played with looked to you for? Ideas? Getting into action? Confidence to take on scary challenges?) Make note of what you're proudest of having accomplished [in school and in jobs]. Match those stories with your differentiating qualities—you'll notice they pair up well."*

Then there is the matter of protecting your business income, sparing yourself being underpaid, or even not being paid at all. Advice here focuses on two complementary aspects: not underpricing your services and, if you're serving individual clients rather than selling a product to a larger audience, always getting in writing a commitment to be paid. Two common and painful early mistakes are being afraid to charge what you're worth, and having disputes over payment in the absence of a contract. I've made a lot of mistakes but, even with long-term trustworthy clients, I've never done a project based only on a verbal agreement or a handshake in my 30-plus years of being my own boss.

On the matter of expectations, several respondents cautioned that it's easy to underestimate how long it will take to ramp up their independent business to a successful level. As one said, *"This is not something to be done between company jobs!"* Some who thought it would take a year or two said it took more like three or four years (obviously dependent on the nature of the business). They prevailed with patience, persistence, and adapting to crosscurrents as they arose. That brings us back to setting aggressive goals as discussed in Lesson 8, but not unrealistic ones.

The final theme on this question was all about boundaries: maintaining boundaries around overwork to protect your health, and to ensure sufficient time to nurture your relationships with family and friends. As a sole practitioner doctor advised, *"You'll likely work harder for yourself than you did for others. Often we have to put work first, but don't often put your loved ones or health second or third. You can lose both that way."* Profound? No. Obvious? Perhaps. Important? Absolutely.

Lest all this advice seem daunting, the aforementioned leadership coach reminded us that for most of us there is likely an ultimate safety net if things don't work out. Her advice: *"Do it. Nothing is forever—you can always go back!"*

### 7. What advice would you have for newly self-employeds to sustain success over the long haul?

Themes:

- Pace yourself
- Be careful how you define productivity
- Reframe how you think about selling (if it's a turn-off to you)
- Make reaching out for advice an ongoing necessity, not just before or during startup
- Stay current, and adapt
- Don't start without financial reserves

- Be careful what you say yes to
- Lapses in integrity and professionalism can be irreparable
- Periodically revisit your initial assumptions

Much as with Question 6, Question 7 was not focused on business strategy advice. I leave that to the many books on how to write a business plan or start a business. Rather, in line with the rest of this book, Questions 6 and 7 solicited input on how to successfully and simultaneously occupy the role of being your own boss and, at the same time, being his/her/their subordinate. So in thinking about the long haul, consider the following commentary as an extension of Lesson 10.

The importance of pacing yourself was already well covered there, but related is the idea of being careful how you define *productivity* for yourself. You'll constantly be judging that. It's too easy to confuse being busy with being productive. Yet productivity often doesn't mean doing more, but rather focusing on less. It's also tempting to think that self-employment guarantees a boost in your productivity when you're no longer attending unnecessary meetings or complying with bureaucratic have-to's. But what is "productive?" As one of my hard-charging entrepreneurial respondents opined, *"I believe it's important to realize that you're not going to be 'productive' 100% of the time, and [to also realize] that that's okay. No one I know was ever 100% productive in an office, either. So, if you can relax and take time to do some of the things you'd do in the office—chat with colleagues [if you have them], have calls with friends unrelated to work, take a little longer at lunch for whatever reason—then do it and don't think twice."*

The first advice that some offered for long-term, sustainable success was about selling yourself. Even some who are very good at it don't like doing it. But when *you* are the business, there's no getting around it. As one consultant said, *"Sell is not a four-letter word. We all do it."* Another: *"Always be selling. Business development is an ongoing part of the job. You cannot stop pipeline development to focus 100% on client work."* Fortunately, a lot of selling isn't 'knocking on doors' (even metaphorically). Some of my respondents, like myself, write articles for publications and blogs—or write books—in their fields of expertise, creating awareness and building credibility. And a sole practitioner psychotherapist reminded us that a lot of other 'selling' is indirect as well: *"Keep planting seeds and know that they will sprout in their own time, not necessarily where you planted them. The energy you put out comes back from unexpected places."*

Reaching out is another theme that lives on long after you start a business. One of my most polymathic respondents, even with her broad range of skills, reported, *"I set up my own virtual board of other independent business owners. These were people with diverse disciplines who could advise me on everything from tax and finance to sustainable business practices and everything in between. Having trusted partners who you can reach out to for their thoughts, as well as redundancy if you are ill or need support, is critical to staying in business, as well as enjoying the journey. We trade time and advise each other on aspects of our businesses."* So, remember that you may also be able to barter with people who have complementary expertise or can act as sounding boards.

Some respondents spoke of how failure to sustain an independent business can simply occur from failure to adapt. When I was employed, my company paid for expensive subscriptions to important publications in my industry, and I often discussed with my staff and peers the developments reported in those publications. So staying current was a regular part of work. But on your own, it's easy to let that slide—whether because you're so busy or not willing to pay for as much information out of your own pocket. As one consultant said, *"A pitfall of running a small independent business is becoming myopic in one's view of the market. It's all too easy to stay on the same path, and miss the nuanced changes in the market or competitive environment. Larger companies have people dedicated to studying trends and making strategic recommendations based on those trends. Smaller firms have to find other ways to stay abreast of what's going on, and how to adapt their value proposition/offer to the market. The two best ways I know of to manage this are asking your clients or customers what kinds of changes they see and how are their needs changing, and finding partner firms to collaborate with that can share information about what they're seeing in the market."*

And then there's always the money. Sustained success can't happen if you run out of it before you're profitable unless you're comfortable borrowing, and even that is a source of stress. A chef starting a sauce business, initially doing everything himself, said, *"Have enough money to fund the first few years without drawing an income. This eliminates a significant amount of financial pressure and also allows all revenues to be put back into building the business. Having savings or an alternate income during the first few years can make all the difference in being able to allow the business to mature to a more stable financial condition."* While service businesses tend to be less capital intensive than product businesses, and usually can generate income sooner, this theme of having a cushion is relevant for all.

Now we turn to two related themes that are things to avoid: saying yes to business that is bad for you, and allowing even minor lapses in professionalism or integrity. We've all been there: the temptation of a project or client that isn't aligned with our values, but the money is good and they are catching you at a time when your income is soft. As one said, *"When you say yes to something be sure it's not out of fear. If you say yes to something that's not really your brand, you may have to say no to something that's a better fit. And it will be harder for others to know what you stand for. If it's not a right fit, let go early—the right thing is right behind it as soon as you stop chasing the wrong thing."*

On a lighter note, one respondent's advice is that if you're going to be working from home, put a lock on the refrigerator! But seriously, I've actually found that for years I have eaten healthier in my home office than I ever did when employed. I can control what's available, make sure it's organic whenever possible, and try to keep unhealthy snacks out of the house (especially after the hundreds of dollars I put into vending machines when I was employed).

## The Good, the Bad, and the Ugly

So that's a boatload of advice from my No Boss compatriots, unfettered and from their hard-won experience. Underneath are many cautionary tales beyond the ones of my own that I've already shared. But when I say that the No Boss journey has absolutely been net positive for me, most everyone on that journey who I have ever talked with agrees. Yes, a few have decided it wasn't for them even after giving it a good long try, and have gone back to collecting that paycheck. They actually seem more happily employed than before their No Boss experiment, having sowed their independent oats and no longer wondering what that would be like. But the overwhelming majority of independent workers I know—even having suffered the slings and arrows of independence along with the joys—would do it again if given the chance to start over. Some would do it differently, including myself as I've acknowledged in previous chapters. But as one said, *"If you can live with uncertainty, and love to learn and grow, it's a great career – because you are creating it."*

And now, after all you've read in these 12 lessons and the many "sub-lessons" embedded in them, if you're ready to start or advance on your own No Boss adventure, please proceed to the Signing Ceremony. It captures the essence and spirit of this book, so it's worth reading even if you're not quite ready to commit. But if or when you are, it will cement—and celebrate—your commitment, and help ensure its success.

\* \* \*

## CODA

──◆──

# Your Signing Ceremony

──◆──

If you've read this far, chances are you're seriously leaning toward independence—or perhaps you're already there. In either case, I hope you're now feeling better prepared for what lies ahead. If you're already bossing yourself around, congratulations on the courage you demonstrated when making the leap. But if you're still standing at the precipice, I remember how it can look like a long way down. To that I say: *look up* and, in contrast, notice the limitlessness above!

To send you off with the wind at your back when your decision is made, the time has come to sign the No Boss Contract found in Lesson 1. Why do I insist on this? Because if someone had offered the same to me more than 30 years ago, and I had signed it and honored it, I would have made far fewer mistakes and realized even greater rewards. And that is what I wish for you. So read the contract again, now that you've absorbed the lessons that came afterwards. Then a ritual signing ceremony is in order.

You may think I'm kidding. I'm not. The No Boss journey should be joyous, and celebrated, just as we celebrate other new beginnings with rituals—from births to weddings. In virtually every culture, rituals are especially important in times of transition and uncertainty. And suffice it to say that the move to independent work, especially if you've been employed for a long period of time, is a huge bucketful of transition and uncertainty. Even an extended period of just thinking seriously about pursuing independent work can put you in what psychologists call a "liminal state"—on the threshold of change but without yet having a clear picture or direction for where you're going. Liminality (derived from the Latin for 'threshold'), as a period of being *in between*, can be an unsettling time to say the least. Psychotherapists use rituals to help people transition from one psychological state to another. It's an understatement to say that controlling your own agenda and bossing yourself around constitute a different psychological state than being employed.

So, what kind of ritual? Sure, you can have a party or maybe just a couple of beers with friends, or a little family dinner celebration. All good. But whether or not you do any of those things, I'm suggesting a *private* ritual that is only you—during which you sign the No Boss Contract in a quiet, sacred moment that is at once celebratory, reflective, hopeful, and, above all, affirmative of your solemn commitment to the principles that will help you succeed. Independent work is a deeply personal decision, deserving a deeply personal ritual. If you're already on your No Boss journey, you're not exempt; think of this as reaffirming your vows, along with some new ones.

Your signing ceremony—your personal affirming ritual, a rite of passage—can be done in just part of an hour, but do it when you're not rushed and can stretch out with it if the spirit moves you. You'll regret having to cut it short. Bring this book and/or a copy of the contract. Bring a journal if you have one, or at least a notepad, as you may well have thoughts during this ritual that you won't want to (or shouldn't) forget.

There is no single right way to structure your ritual. But here's a backbone starter agenda for you to modify to whatever you think will serve you best in the same spirit.

1. Find a quiet room with no distractions (or you may prefer a beautiful quiet spot in the great outdoors where you can be alone, when the weather is accommodating). Turn off your phone (or any electronic devices, unless you feel it would be helpful to have some very

softly playing *non-verbal* music that is special to you in a calming or inspirational way).

2. If inside, light a candle (or several). Get relaxed—take a few deep breaths and hold each one for three seconds before exhaling slowly. Or if you already practice deep breathing, do that in your usual way.

3. Take a few minutes to reflect on how you got to this moment—the journey that brought you here. Appreciate that you are probably where you're supposed to be right now. It's *not* a time to focus on regrets, but rather to know that everything you've done in your work life—the pleasures and the pain (our two great teachers)—has prepared you for this moment.

4. Then take a few minutes to reflect on your vision of success and your dreams and aspirations; some will be specific to your intended independent work, and some may be related to the larger life that independent work enables. Revel in those thoughts, but also remind yourself not to expect too much too soon. Aggressive stretch goals are encouraged; wildly unrealistic ones may only set you up for disappointment or even premature abandonment of independence.

5 Carefully re-read, in this moment, the No Boss Contract. It should remain in force for as long as you work independently. As you re-read, pay attention to which covenants give you the most pause. Make a note of those for future deep examination of where the anxieties lay, as a step toward developing strategies (and using the ones in this book) to mitigate them. But think of them as surmountable. They likely are!

6. *Sign.*

7. Now, take a moment of deep *intention*—intending with conviction that the future you envision is the future you will have, knowing deep down that the rewards,

tangible and intangible, will be worth the effort and the risks.

8. Congratulate yourself! (If you can boss yourself around, you're certainly capable of congratulating yourself. This is a celebration!)

9. Optional: close out the ritual with a brief moment of whatever your personal version of prayer looks like. (We need not be religious in the traditional sense to invite and accept divine intervention, wherever the divine may come from.)

10. Emerge hopeful, energetic, and confident!

With your ritual completed, know that you follow in hallowed independent footsteps that have changed the world. Historian Thomas Cahill has a wonderful passage in his acclaimed book *The Gifts of the Jews*, in which he explores the extraordinary significance of Avram (Abraham) setting out for Canaan some 4,000 years ago. Cahill posits that Abraham didn't actually know where he was going, only that his God had told him to "go forth" on a journey of no return to an unknown land that would somehow ultimately become a great nation. The passage I refer to couldn't be more relevant to the No Boss journey:

> *"So, 'wayyelekh Avram' ('Avram went')—two of the boldest words in all literature. ... Out of ancient humanity, which from the beginnings of its consciousness has read its eternal verities in the stars, comes a party traveling by no known compass. Out of the human race, which knows in its bones that all its striving must end in death, comes a leader who says he has been given an impossible promise. Out of mortal imagination comes a dream of something new, something better, something yet to happen, something—in the future."*

Abraham *went*. That's the point. What if he hadn't? And he was 75 years old when he made this perilous journey into the great unknown. So no excuses for us!

## Coda • 143

With this, I bid you a fond farewell with my sincerest wishes for good fortune. When there are disappointments, try to transport yourself back to your signing ceremony and remember how you felt as it concluded. Remember the confidence. Remember the intention. Repeat it often. (Daily is good, especially early on.) Lean on this book in whatever ways it may be helpful, and know that its author is rooting for you, cheering you on from the sidelines when you *go forth*!

* * *

## ACKNOWLEDGEMENTS AND GRATITUDE

I dedicated my last book to my wife, Elaine, as "my anchor in the wind." She still is. An independent worker herself as a psychotherapist and life coach, she has taught me much of what I know about mental health and personal growth—two pillars on which successful long-term independent work rests.

My thanks to all the other talented, smart, and lovely people who have informed this book with their thoughts and career journeys. Among them are Janet Beach, Kim Bennett, Richard Black, Scott Campbell, Amy Davis, Ron Donovan, Ethan Dulsky, Charles Fleishman, Glenn Fleishman, Lee Franklin, Marijo Franklin, Ralph Golan, Mike Lisagor, Gail McCormick, Howard Powers, Mitchell Pumpian, Andrew Salzman, David Thompson, Susi Watson, and Steve Weyer. I was very fortunate to have editing help from the eagle eyes of Nancy Morgan, and the interior book design expertise of Vladimir Verano at VerVolta Press.

I also thank the many clients I have had the privilege of serving and knowing and learning from in some of the most exciting and innovative companies in the world. You know who you are. You have modeled successful employment, and shown how the right role in the right company can be a better choice for so many people than independent work—and how the wrong role or the wrong company can be redeemed by the courage to make a change, or even change yourself.

To my coaches, thank you for the wisdom you have imparted to help me keep my own No Boss journey on the rails all these years, and for holding me accountable to principles and goals. Your fingerprints are on this book in countless ways. And to my coaching clients, thank you for your trust in me and your inspiring dedication to improving your work lives. I have certainly learned from you as well.

Finally, a shout-out to all my bosses, both the great and terrible ones. The great ones taught me how to be a better boss, first to others and then to myself, and the terrible ones unwittingly helped push me into the arms of independent work sooner than I might have otherwise gone. It's been a great ride. Thank you all. ♦

# ABOUT THE AUTHOR

STEVEN CRISTOL is a business consultant, career coach, former Fortune 50 executive, singer/songwriter, inventor, and author whose business books have been published in eleven languages. He is the founder of Strategic Harmony® Partners, a business strategy consultancy.

Having previously worked for nine bosses in five companies large and small, including serving as Vice President of Marketing Communications for Pacific Bell (now AT&T) and chief marketing officer for a rapid-growth music technology company acquired by Time Warner, he has sustained independent work for more than 30 years. As a sole proprietor he has advised more than 50 innovative companies ranging from global market leaders to Silicon Valley technology startups. More information about Steven, and the book, at www.noboss.me.